Photographing People for Stock

Photographing People for Stock

Nancy Brown

with Michael O'Connor

AMPHOTO
an imprint of Watson-Guptill Publications/New York

Nancy Brown has been a commercial photographer in New York City for seventeen years. Prior to that, she was a model for twenty years. Specializing in people, she has clients worldwide, including advertising agencies, magazines, public relations firms, pharmaceutical agencies, book publishers, and design firms. The Image Bank has handled her stock photographs for fifteen years.

Nancy gives lectures and seminars around the country, and has taught at The Maine Photographic Workshop, The Appalachian Workshop, and The Tahoe Workshop. She also runs summer workshops out of her studio in New York City. Author of many magazine articles on photography, she has also written *Photographing People for Advertising* (Amphoto 1986). Her two daughters live in West Palm and Boca Raton, Florida, where they assist her on stock shoots.

Editorial concept by Robin Simmen
Edited by Carl Rosen
Designed by Areta Buk
Graphic production by Ellen Greene

Copyright © 1993 by Nancy Brown
First published in 1993 by Amphoto,
an imprint of Watson-Guptill Publications,
a division of BPI Communications, Inc.,
1515 Broadway, New York, NY 10036

Library of Congress Cataloging-in-Publication Data

Brown, Nancy (Nancy Walker)
    Photographing people for stock : how to take photos that sell
again and again / Nancy Brown.
        p.   cm.
    Includes bibliographical references.
    ISBN 0-8174-5500-0. — ISBN 0-8174-5501-9 (pbk.)
    1. Stock photography—Handbooks, manuals, etc. 2. Photographs—
Marketing—Handbooks, manuals, etc.   I. Title.
TR690.6.B75 1993
770'.68—dc20   92-43501
                                                        CIP

Manufactured in Singapore

1 2 3 4 5 6 7 8 9 / 00 99 98 97 96 95 94 93

THIS BOOK IS DEDICATED TO ESTER JOHNSTON,
WITH SPECIAL THANKS TO SHARLAND BLANCHARD
AND LAURA STILES

Contents

Introduction

"THE BEST APPROACH TO STOCK IS TO CREATE PHOTOGRAPHS IN YOUR OWN STYLE, WITH SOMEONE ELSE'S NEEDS IN MIND."

Photographing People for Stock is about taking commercial photographs of people that will sell around the world, again and again, for years. This book will show you how good money can be made from taking photographs at times, in places, and with people of your own choosing. Fortunately, I've had an exciting and fulfilling career in stock photography for many years. Since I am often asked about my work in the field, I decided to write this book. In it, I describe the kind of photographs I take, what goes into setting up stock shoots, and how my photographs of people make money for me. By sharing my insights with you, I hope to show that you can enjoy photographing people while earning money by selling your images as stock.

A brief definition is in order: The term *stock* refers to existing, as opposed to *assigned,* photographs. A stock photograph is an image taken in advance of any particular need for it. The market for commercial stock photography is gigantic. Stock photographs are used around the world for advertisements, magazines and newspapers, textbooks, real-estate brochures, travel posters, greeting cards, drugstore flyers, toothpaste coupons, cereal boxes, postcards, souvenirs, and many other purposes. Not all the photographs you see published in these media are stock photographs, but many are. For example, in a multi-image advertisement, a picture of a particular brand of toothpaste propped against its box is probably not a stock photograph; the picture is too specific. But the picture of a couple frolicking in the winter scene above the toothpaste is likely to be a stock photograph. And that incredible picture of a Norwegian fjord on the poster in your travel agency's window is virtually certain to be a stock photograph.

Introduction

In many situations, stock photographs offer advertisers and publishers a number of advantages over assigned photographs. One advantage is that buying an image from stock is frequently cheaper than assigning someone to photograph the same thing. Another advantage, perhaps more important, is that buyers know exactly what a stock picture looks like before they spend a single penny on it. No matter how good photographers are, they can't guarantee that amazing clouds will appear over a remote fjord at sunset next Tuesday. It is a lot safer for a client, such as an airline seeking an image for a poster, to use a great picture that is already on hand.

Though it is common to refer to a stock photograph as having been *sold* to a client (and I use that term in this book), it is rare for a stock photograph to change hands as you would sell a car. What actually happens is that specific reproduction rights in a stock photograph are licensed to a client for a fee. The transaction is more like renting a car. A client rents a car for a defined period of time. The longer the rental, the higher the price.

In exchange for payment for your photograph, you grant the client the right to reproduce the photograph in a very specific way for a limited period of time (usually a year). The photograph itself remains in your possession, and you may license other uses of the same picture to other clients. Multiple sales are the best way to

make money in stock photography. The right to grant the use of your photograph simultaneously to several clients makes stock photography a viable industry, and it is one of the major reasons why stock photography is often less expensive for clients than assigned photography. This whole concept is based in copyright law, a subject too complicated for this book to explore in depth. Basically, the law states that there is a virtually unlimited *bundle of rights* contained in any photograph and that the person who took the photograph may parcel out these rights in any way he or she chooses.

Let me give you an example of how copyright works in stock photography. If a real-estate developer in Florida buys a year's right to use your picture of a couple playing tennis for the cover of a sales brochure, you retain the right to license the same picture to a tennis magazine published in New York, a travel agency in Alaska, a sporting-goods store in London, a country club in Brazil, and a new nightclub in Tokyo. In a year and a day, you could legally license the rights to print a poster of the same picture to another real-estate developer in Florida, even if he or she was right across the street from your first client. Professional ethics, however, would rule out such an action. If you are going to succeed in stock photography, you need repeat business from clients. To achieve this, you must keep your clients happy.

Introduction

The stock-photography industry is almost as large and diverse as the market for stock pictures. However, the most common way that stock photographs get into your local newspaper's Sunday magazine or onto the front of your shopping cart is through *stock-photo agencies*. These agencies (sometimes called *picture libraries*) file millions of photographs, usually from many different photographers. There are many such agencies around the world (the largest, most respected stock-photo agencies are members of the Picture Agency Council of America—see page 142 for more information about them). Some represent the files of only a few photographers; some work only in local markets or special subject areas; and some are huge, with numerous offices in many countries.

Clients contact stock-photo agencies to find photographs of the subjects they need, and the agencies constantly promote their files and services to the kinds of clients who buy photographs. Many of the larger agencies periodically publish and distribute catalogs showcasing selected images from their files. I've found that the photographs published in agency catalogs usually generate multiple sales.

Almost all stock-photo agencies work on consignment. In other words, the photographer places pictures in the agency's files, and the agency tries to market them. If any of the photographs sell, the agency and the photographer split the income (percentages vary). Normally, the photographer is paid after the client pays the agency. This means that it can take years from the time the photographer submits a photograph before any income on it is received, even if it sells. In my experience, it is unusual to receive income on a picture in fewer than six months.

Agencies and individual photographers price stock photographs according to how a client plans to use a photograph and the length of time a client uses it. Be aware that the same image could be worth ten thousand or five hundred dollars, depending on how it is used. For example, it would cost a client much more to use a stock image in an ongoing advertising campaign than in a one-shot flyer. Some categories of usage (high- to low-end) are:

- Consumer ads
- Billboards
- Television commercials
- Pharmaceutical ads
- POP (point-of-purchase) displays
- FSI (free-standing inserts)
- Posters
- Brochures
- Editorial
- Audio-visual
- Textbooks

Each use has its own price range. If you don't know what to charge, call a few stock agencies and get their pricelists. You can also get advice on price ranges by asking other photographers who sell stock. Important factors that are often overlooked in pricing are the difficulty and expense that went into a photograph's production. Be sure to consider these costs to you when you license usage. Whatever you charge, you have to be comfortable with your prices and see that your efforts are profitable.

Many professional photographers market their own stock pictures and files. Some sell to a large client base, in which case having a paid staff helps. Others sell to relatively fewer but more consistent clients. And to be honest, some photographers fail miserably trying to sell their own stock photos. Marketing stock is a difficult job in addition to creating photographs.

sixty-four offices all over the world. The Image Bank pioneered the sale of stock photographs to advertising agencies and for high-end editorial use. I have been with The Image Bank since it was founded nearly twenty years ago.

Being with such an agency is obviously critical to making a good income from stock photography. Finding a good stock-photo agency, and getting it to represent and market your photographs, is an involved subject. Working successfully with an agency is also complicated. There are many variables, particularly in the areas of talent, how hard you want to work, how much money you want to invest, and how patient you are.

I wish I could be more specific about how to get an agency to represent you, but that would fill an entirely different book. The best advice I can give you here is to suggest that you do a lot of research in the field, beginning with the publications listed in the appendix of this book. I also recommend joining a trade association and talking to every professional photographer and art director with whom you come in contact.

There is much more I could tell you about the stock-photo industry, but this book is about making photographs of people to sell as stock. You can know everything there is to know about marketing stock photographs, but without making the right types of photographs, your knowledge won't do you any good. So let's get on with the subject.

Most of my stock photography is sold through an agency called The Image Bank, but occasionally I sell stock photographs directly to clients. My direct sales are of photographs not in The Image Bank and don't resemble their pictures. My own files are filled with shots lacking model releases. When I sell one of these, I pay the model a fee. The Image Bank will only accept released material. If a client goes to The Image Bank first and then comes to me for the same or similar photograph, I am bound by contract to send them back to The Image Bank.

The Image Bank is the world's largest and most successful stock-photo agency. The company has

Introduction

The commercial stock-photography industry is barely twenty-five years old. It is just beginning to enter maturity, even though the industry as a whole is estimated to generate sales in excess of two hundred million dollars a year. As stock photography matures, the pictures available in all markets are becoming increasingly sophisticated. Clients for stock photography now expect more refined, interpretive, even artistic photographs.

It used to be true that the vast majority of photographs available as stock had a certain artificial, two-dimensional feeling to them. Although technically perfect (sometimes almost too much so), many stock photographs lacked what can be called "emotional depth." Everyone in early stock photographs was always smiling, the sun was always shining, and the settings were always perfectly clean. Everything was in sharp focus; not only were there flowers on every table, but not a single one was wilting. As a result, many stock photographs simply didn't reflect real life.

In the past two years or so, however, the type of imagery available as stock has undergone an enormous visual change. Almost overnight, the basic aesthetic of stock photography has radically evolved, and today there is definitely a "new look" in stock photography. The new look is "looser"; it conveys a freer, more fluid sense than older

stock images. Instead of being highly structured, with each model seemingly rooted in place, many stock photographs now have a snapshot-like quality. They appear to be true slices of life, captured rather than constructed. Some people describe the new look as being a so-called editorial quality. Certain figures in the pictures might be out of focus. There might be blur where there is movement. A few shadows, or someone with hair out of place, might appear—and not everyone is always smiling.

Defining this new look in stock photography is difficult. The best way to understand it is to compare the catalogs published by major stock agencies today with those published only a few years ago—the trend becomes obvious immediately. In addition to the highly stylized color photographs of the past, today's catalogs contain many black-and-white images and pictures taken on a tilt or with the frame cutting into part of one of the models. Many of the photographs in this book have this new look, including the ones shown here.

When asked to distill into a rule of thumb what I consider the best approach to photographing people for stock, I say it is "creating photographs in your own style, with someone else's needs in mind." That sounds simple, but it actually involves several different points. First, there is the issue of *creating*. In my experience,

successful stock photographs are not "taken," but made, or "created." This is an important distinction: You *take* photographs of a scene or situation that already exists without your influence. When you *create* photographs, you set up and arrange the situation or scene, then record what you have fabricated with a camera. That is how I take stock photographs.

Originally, most stock photographs were actually *outtakes* from assignments—photographs that weren't used by the original client for any number of reasons— or they were pictures taken simply for the purpose of recording an existing thing or place. As the market for stock became more sophisticated, and the money flowed more freely, commercial photographers realized they could increase their sales in this area by shooting specifically for stock.

I approach my stock shoots with as much attention to detail and determination to get great pictures as my paid assignments from major advertising agencies. My stock shoots are fully planned and developed productions, carefully organized so that the location, props, wardrobe, talent, and crew are all perfect. As much, if not more, work goes into setting up the production as goes into taking the actual photographs.

The second point in my formula for success is summed up in the phrase "in your own style." Today, art directors want pictures of a

particular subject with a little something extra—some flair and distinct feeling—in other words, with style. Photographic style is difficult to define but usually appears when you photograph subjects you like and know something about, and when you create pictures that mirror your personal outlook on life and the world. Honest photographs are the ones most often selected for the larger, better, and more lucrative uses.

I truly like people, so it is part of my style to take pictures of people. I also have an extremely positive outlook and attitude, and I believe in enjoying life. That feeling comes through in my pictures (even if sometimes I have to work at producing it), and you could say that is another element of my style. I doubt, however, that I'd be particularly good at taking pictures of buildings or race cars.

Other elements of photographic style are more literal, such as choices of clothing, the colors that attract you, the angles you use most often in your photographs, and, of course, any special techniques you favor. I like bright colors, and I love white, so you see many bright colors and lots of white in my pictures. I love a soft and romantic feeling, and an element of fantasy, so I frequently work with a diffusion filter. Also, I really enjoy using high-speed film for enhanced grain. Those techniques are definitely aspects of my own particular photographic style.

Introduction

After you discover your own personal photographic style, it is important to be true to it. Not only will your pictures be much better and sell better, but you'll also be happier with them, which is very important. You may not want to believe it, and on the surface it may not seem to make sense, but if you try to take photographs in too many styles, you won't produce good images. Another photographer's successful approach is probably not for you. If you don't shoot pictures in your own style, the results will look like copies, weak seconds compared to the work of the original photographer. Most clients are savvy enough to spot a copied style and will simply opt for the real thing. Again, once you have discovered your own photographic style, develop and be true to it.

The third part of my philosophy, and the real key to creating successful stock photographs from a marketing viewpoint, is summarized in the phrase "with someone else's needs in mind." The whole reason the stock-photography industry exists is to fulfill the needs of advertisers and publishers. It is a service industry. The photographs that sell as stock solve problems for someone or satisfy a very specific need.

Knowing, or anticipating, the needs of someone you've never talked to or met is not easy. There is no foolproof way to learn how to anticipate your client's needs. Generally, it takes years of experience before a professional photographer grasps this part of stock photography. For example, it has taken me years to begin to have a basic idea of market direction, and I've had help from many people.

When shooting for stock, keep in mind that a potential client might want to use your picture along with other people's photographs.

Frequently, clients use stock shots as backgrounds for other images (particularly photographs of products), and often they print headlines or copy over them (which is why photographs taken against a white seamless-paper background are so saleable).

On a shoot, always try to take some photographs that include space for clients to drop-in type. Don't come in close to the subject on every shot or frame all your pictures too tightly. When taking a vertical picture that you think might work well as a cover page, be sure to leave some space at the top where a headline or title could go. And when you shoot horizontal photographs, isolate the main point of interest in half of the frame. This is a classic, dynamic composition for a photograph. Such photographs work extremely well when reproduced across two pages of a magazine (left) because the half of the frame not taken up by the center of interest is perfect for superimposing other pictures or type.

Becoming a successful stock photographer takes time and experience, and it is quite a challenge. The challenge, though, is one of the things that makes it so personally satisfying when (and I must say "if") you finally succeed. I wrote *Photographing People for Stock* to tell you as much as possible about what I've learned from experience in order to make the process easier and the road shorter for you. Hopefully, you'll enjoy your photography more, too.

COURTESY *VICTORIA*. *VICTORIA* IS A PUBLICATION OF HEARST MAGAZINES, A DIVISION OF THE HEARST CORPORATION

A Few Basic Tips

What follows is a list of my most basic rules of thumb when shooting for stock. I hope they will help you make better-selling pictures and have more fun doing so.

- Always shoot both horizontal and vertical pictures so your images can be used as many ways as possible. (If you are shooting in a rush because of fading light, scheduling, or some other reason, shoot only horizontals. You can always crop a vertical from a horizontal, but not vice versa.)

- Leave room in the photograph for type. (If you think a photograph might work for the cover of a magazine or book, leave room for type in the upper half of the photo.)

- Don't use just one type of framing when you cover a situation. Move in closer and out farther, so that you get headshots, portraits, and three-quarter views, as well as full figures.

- Use brightly colored clothes and props, especially when photographing outdoors. (This depends on the subject and mood of your photograph, of course, but overall, photographs with bright colors seem to sell best.)

- Try to coordinate the colors of the clothes, props, and furniture in your photographs, both in the studio and on location. Pictures with a definite color scheme are generally more marketable.

- Have your models look at, and relate to, each other more than to the camera.

- Remember to photograph your models from behind and in profile whenever possible. This makes the people in your pictures less specifically identifiable. Or, to put it another way, it allows viewers to impose imagined features on your models.

- Always get signed releases for anything recognizable in your pictures—locations, pets, unusual pieces of property—as well as from models.

- Be ready to spend money to produce good stock photographs. At the same time, however, buy clothing and props with good, clean, classic lines. This will permit their repeated use, and your pictures won't date as quickly.

- Continually look through various publications (including those you wouldn't normally buy) to see what kind of pictures are selling and what styles of lighting, styling, talent, and so forth are being used in advertisements.

- Always plan your shoots. And always shoot enough film to cover the situations thoroughly. When you don't plan enough, things always seem to go wrong, and too little film means you can't take full advantage of situations when they go perfectly. In my experience, you can't plan too much or use too much film.

- Be flexible once a shoot starts. Go with the flow of the models and the situation as it develops. Frequently, being spontaneous leads to better pictures.

- Always have a positive attitude, and work to keep people's energy and enthusiasm at a peak. Doing so will give you a competitive edge and make your shoots much more enjoyable for you and everyone else involved.

Lifestyle Photography

Shooting lifestyles for stock is a favorite self-assignment. I take a lot of lifestyle pictures, and fortunately, lifestyle photography is one of the best-selling types of stock photography. A *lifestyle photograph* is a "slice of life," one instant out of a particular person's day captured on film. Lifestyle photographs often show groups of people in casual situations, comfortably dressed and enjoying life. They focus on people having fun, which is what makes them so much fun for me.

Although lifestyle photographs include people, they shouldn't be confused with portraits. In a lifestyle picture, the subject isn't a person or even a group of people, but an enjoyable moment or a particularly fun event, such as a skating party among best friends on a lovely frozen lake in bright sunshine. Most lifestyle pictures emphasize surroundings as well as people. They provide a glimpse of the things owned by the people in the picture, the places they live in or visit, and the activities that occupy them. To create stock lifestyle photographs that will sell for many years to come, you should use locations and props that aren't tied too closely to a specific place or fashion.

Glance through the pages of virtually any magazine and you'll see scores of lifestyle photographs. In advertisements, popular lifestyle scenarios—people frolicking on the beach, families hiking in the woods, couples chatting in cafés—are used to sell a wide variety of products, from health insurance to decaffeinated coffee. When the product being advertised appears in the picture, it is reasonable to assume that the photograph was taken on assignment. But when the product is superimposed on the picture, somewhere else on the page, or perhaps not shown at all (as in a real-estate advertisement), the picture is likely to be a stock photograph. That means a stock photographer made money from what was probably a very pleasant day of self-assigned shooting.

Lifestyle Photography

One key to shooting lifestyle for stock is creating a "real" feeling in your pictures. In other words, the pictures should look natural—not posed, set up, or fake—which isn't necessarily easy to accomplish. There are no hard-and-fast rules for making "real" pictures, but using healthy, happy-looking models who look more ordinary than superattractive can help. Stunning or extreme-looking people don't work because they look like models. Glamorous models tend to become the central focus of a picture, overpowering the real subject. Remember, the subject of a lifestyle photograph is a slice of life, a situation that conveys a feeling. When clients are advertising something like breakfast cereal, they probably want a picture that appeals to a broad range of people and imparts feelings of family, health, security, and home. A woman with legs up to her neck, or a man who could double for James Bond, would impart an unduly exotic feeling and certainly distract from the client's product.

The need for subjects who look real is actually an advantage for the stock photographer. It means that you can work with attractive, healthy-looking friends, family, and acquaintances rather than professionals, although I generally use professionals. The subjects, however, must fit the character of the situation you wish to portray,

and there are plenty of professional models and actors who are natural-looking types.

Just as you need people who fit the situation, the props and clothes you use should be realistic. They can be a little more elegant or expensive than everyday life, but not totally inaccessible. (There are always exceptions in photography. Some stock lifestyle photographs featuring very expensive cars have sold quite well.) As mentioned above, clothing and props with classic lines and timeless styling are generally best. They don't date a picture as quickly as trendy items, and a classically styled image can be published in many countries without looking foreign to the viewers.

Another key to shooting a successful lifestyle photograph for stock is interaction between the people in the photograph. Interaction not only makes the situation and picture appear more real, but it adds something in terms of mood and emotion. And remember, those are the elements many clients want when buying stock photographs. Nothing looks more stilted, phony, and boring than a row of people standing stiffly and staring straight at the camera—and nothing sells worse. Without a feeling of liveliness, a picture isn't a lifestyle photograph (though it may have value as some sort of document).

If you can help your models (professionals or amateurs) to interact in a natural manner, better pictures will result. An atmosphere of friendship and mutual trust makes models feel relaxed, happy,

and confident. People who are touching, smiling at each other, laughing at a mutual joke, wrestling and roughhousing, make all the difference. As a photographer, you should direct the shoot and set the tone of the situation; be honest, friendly, and relaxed. Let the models know that you won't take advantage of them and that you want them to interact.

The way people are grouped in a picture—the way they are bending, leaning, and touching—is what produces the impression that they are interacting and relating to each other. Interaction, however, doesn't necessarily mean that no one should ever look at the camera. In fact, in many of my pictures, some, or even all, of the people are looking at the camera. Eye contact can create a feeling of intimacy between the viewer and the people in the picture.

One way to make lifestyle pictures look real and to help models interact is to develop a *storyline*. A storyline doesn't have to be complicated. It can be as simple as "a beautiful day in the country" or "the family's summer picnic." (You'll see both of these storylines in the next few pages.) Have the models act out a storyline as you photograph them. In fact, the best lifestyle pictures always tell a story; or, perhaps more accurately, they hint at a story, appearing to be a single moment captured from a continuing situation. Happy and upbeat stories can enliven everyone on a shoot, resulting in better pictures and more enjoyment for everyone involved.

All-American Family

Good, healthy, happy-looking family situations sell quite well as stock, so I decided to produce and photograph a family and location that looked thoroughly "all-American." I wanted to show traditional, American-looking houses and locations, so I went to nearby Connecticut (I work in New York) and drove around until I found the perfect location. I then contacted the owner of the site to get permission to use the property for commercial photography, paid the owner a location fee of 150 dollars, and received a signed property release.

To sell photographs for commercial uses, you must secure permission to include any property or people in them that are recognizable. Obviously, you have to obtain releases from the models, but *property* is a broad category that includes cars—particularly unusual cars—as well as buildings. If you don't obtain a property release, the owner of the property can make a legal claim when the picture is published in an advertisement. This means that no intelligent client is going to buy the rights to use that picture without a release. You don't necessarily need releases for photographs to be used editorially in a magazine or book, but I always secure, and pay for, signed releases whenever I conduct a shoot. Paying something, even a dollar, makes the release entirely valid and means the

property owner has no claim for further reimbursement. My stock house demands that I label all my slides for release status. If your goal is to be a professional stock photographer, get releases.

I put this "family" together with the help of Connecticut model agent Ester Johnston. I knew that I wanted Molly, a model I had photographed many times before, to be the "mom," but I also needed a "dad" and two children: an older boy and younger girl. The girl had to have light hair, and the dad and son had to have similar coloring. Ester and I put together a perfect group, although none of the models were, in fact, related. On the day of the shoot, I drove to Connecticut in my van with one assistant, Sharland. Molly came with us from New York. J.D. (the "dad") and David and Shauna, the two children, along with their real parents, met us at the location. This was my first time working with J.D. and Shauna (the little girl), but it certainly wasn't my last—they were great!

At my request, the models brought wardrobes appropriate to the location, and I brought along brightly colored clothing and props (blankets, baskets, flowers, ropes, and pumpkins). Bright colors are trademarks of my style. Never underestimate the effectiveness of color and props. Bring a lot of props to a shoot— they make situations look more real by fleshing them out, they improve the models' mood, and you never know how they might inspire you photographically.

All-American Family

The weather that day was absolutely perfect. It was so beautiful outdoors that we only shot inside the house on the property once at the end of the day. The rest of the time we worked in the front yard. Most of the shots were backlit (with the sun behind the models), and we used two portable flex-fill reflectors (collapsible reflectors that "fill" a subject with reflected light) to add light to the front of the scenes and the models' faces. (Backlight makes a model's hair glow and helps separate the models from the background. Fill light softens a model's face and is more flattering than direct sunlight.) The boy's real father asked for something to do, and so we taught him to use a flex-fill reflector; he handled it perfectly.

Everything went quite smoothly, and when the kids wanted a break, I photographed Molly and J.D. as a couple (see page 22, bottom). I had a shooting plan, but as usual I was very flexible. When something unexpectedly good happens with my models and the light, I drop my plan and we go with the flow.

I used my Nikon F4 camera and an 80-200mm lens all day. The film was Ektachrome 100 Plus. (After the shoot, I clipped a roll from each different situation and had it test-processed normally. Normal processing worked perfectly, and the results were fine.) We worked very hard for four hours before losing the light. Everyone kept up a great energy level and had fun. The pictures reflect this, and two shots from that day have sold already. All in all, it was a perfect stock day!

An Ethnic Flavor

This series of pictures was shot at the suggestion of The Image Bank. America is a fascinating melting pot of different races, ethnic groups, and cultures. Stock agencies receive many requests for high-quality pictures of attractive people who are distinctly ethnic in appearance. Such images are clearly in demand by companies wishing to advertise certain products or to appeal to specific markets here in the United States. Less obvious to you, perhaps, is the demand overseas for photographs of ethnic models.

In order to maximize your sales as a stock photographer, you have to be aware of the huge markets for photographs outside of America. Many of those markets, particularly in South America and Asia, are growing at a much faster rate than the more developed American and European markets.

At this point in my career, nearly 75 percent of my income from stock photography comes from sales outside of the United States. Granted, some of my pictures sell overseas because they have a very American look, but many others sell because they could have been taken in the countries where they are published. One of the advantages to working in America is that you don't need to travel to

South America or the Far East to find models, props, and settings that'll look appropriate for those markets. Remember, sales and success come from "creating pictures in your style, but with other people's needs in mind."

I decided to produce a series of shoots of an attractive Latino couple in lifestyle situations. Working with Mauro and Daisy, the two models, was a real pleasure. They came from different modeling agencies, but they worked together perfectly and looked great in a number of different settings. They are real professionals. A first set of pictures was done outdoors, near Daisy's house in Brooklyn. Although I had a number of situations in mind before we shot these casual pictures, we also worked where the light and the mood took us. The bicycle picture (left) was taken in direct sunlight, while the picnic shot (below) was taken in the shade under a gorgeous old tree. Both photographs were shot with Ektachrome 100 Plus. In both cases, the sunlight was primarily behind the models, while reflected light from flex-fill reflectors lit the scenes from the front. I love the way the sun backlighting Daisy's lovely hair makes it glow in the bicycle picture.

An Ethnic Flavor

Later in the day, I moved the shoot to my studio to take some pictures of Daisy and Mauro in more formal clothing. The storyline I gave them involved an office or living-room situation. You can imagine the numerous commercial uses for these pictures and the many products they could be used to advertise. The indoor pictures were a great success, and I expect them to sell very well in many countries for years to come. I particularly like the picture of Mauro next to the fluted column (right). It has the sort of moody, unstructured quality that is becoming popular in stock photography. You could say that shadows, along with an impression of movement and spontaneity, are part of the new look in stock photography. Compare the feeling of this picture to the more traditional superclean, bright quality of the bicycle pictures, and you'll see what I mean.

Three Generations Relaxing

Among the best-selling stock photographs are clean, crisp pictures of attractive families having fun and engaged in healthy activities that include three generations. I decided to travel to Connecticut again (I love Connecticut!) to shoot pictures of a "family." This time, I made plans to photograph several different locations and also do some shots showing "grandparents."

I wanted these pictures to be less stylized—more "real" and believable, and less "perfect"—than those made during the "All-American family" shoot. Still, this intergenerational shoot was carefully thought out and planned. I wanted some shots of tennis and boating (or yacht club) situations, as well as a nursery and a park setting, so I went to Connecticut in search of locations the week before the shoot. Matt (the "father"), who is a terrific model and always helpful, suggested a marina we could use, and I found the ideal tennis courts and nursery. This time, I didn't have to pay for property releases. Instead, I traded some slides to the nursery, the tennis club, and the marina in exchange for releases.

The shoot went according to my schedule. The first half of the day, my assistant, Sharland, and I worked with just the "parents" as a couple for the tennis shots and the picnic photographs at the nursery. We also photographed the more casual situations at the marina.

Three Generations Relaxing

The Chitwoods, the older couple who play the grandparents in these pictures, suggested their daughter's pool as a location. It was beautiful, the furniture was perfect, and she was very happy to sign a release.

After lunch, we went to the pool and added the two "grandparents" and the children. Late in the day, we went back to the marina for the photographs of the younger couple dressed more formally. We brought along clothes for everyone, but in most of the shots the models wore their own clothes (of the type I had requested). I just added bright towels or props to the pictures here and there for some spots of color.

the two "parents" together and each individually; the "father" with the "son," with the "daughter," and with both children; and the "mother" with just the "daughter." The locations were ideal, the models perfect, and it made sense to shoot as many saleable images as possible. I can't tell you enough how important it is to provide potential clients with a wide range of choices in format and cropping, in expressions and groupings. Shoot as many variations as possible to increase the chance that you'll have the picture that is just perfect for their needs.

In the picnic pictures on this page, as in the tennis pictures (see page 30), notice that I photographed the models not only from the front, but also from behind. This significantly increases the possibility of sales overseas because the models aren't immediately recognizable as nationals from a particular country. This type of picture also works as a "mood" picture, rather than one in which a specific activity is highlighted. It is interesting to note that while many of these shots are certain to sell very well as stock, the picture of the Chitwoods alone may become the best-selling image of all of them. Realistic images of older couples are extremely popular, and this picture has a very tender, loving feel.

In general, I tried for a casual, highly believable quality in these pictures. When clients request a real look, however, they don't mean algae in the pool or drab clothing. They still want a slightly idealized version of life, but not one so pristine and perfect as to be completely unbelievable. There is a fine line between the real and ideal in pictures, but it is an obvious line, and with practice you'll be able to discern it quickly.

Throughout the day, I shot many variations of each situation, as I always do. I went through lots of film taking vertical shots, horizontals, close-up headshots, and full figures. I photographed

Focus on Women

"TAKE ADVANTAGE OF A WOMAN'S CHARACTER. YOU CAN CHANGE HER MAKEUP AND CLOTHING, BUT DON'T FIGHT HER PERSONALITY—LET IT SHINE THROUGH!"

Photographing women is my specialty. It is also a type of photography that sells very well as stock. Surprisingly few photographers specialize in stock photography of real-looking, energetic women in believable, present-day situations. Focusing on women is, however, relatively easy to do if you have the ideas, enthusiasm, and a basic understanding of the market, as well as the right models.

Women are great subjects because there are so many types of photographs you can take of them. You can dress the same woman in a wide array of outfits to create a remarkable range of feelings in your pictures, to say nothing of the effects you can achieve with makeup. You can't do the same with men, and certainly not with children. Older couples, too, provide fewer options from a photographic and stylistic viewpoint.

I work repeatedly with the same women as models. As a result, we have developed a rapport, a way of understanding each other almost automatically and working together smoothly. I also know immediately which model would work best for a particular situation. You might think that it is a good idea to use a number of models for variety. However, I find that it is much more efficient, and easier, to work with someone I already know well—it takes time to learn each new model's professional strengths, weaknesses, and idiosyncrasies!

Composure, or the ability to look "at home" in many photographic situations, is probably a model's most important quality. The logistics of shooting stock mean that you must set up and cover several situations with the same models during the course of a single day. Models who can strike an appropriate look anywhere are thus your best choice for stock, not high-fashion models. Women with very unusual or extraordinarily beautiful looks tend to dominate photographs, overpowering the product or service the client wishes to advertise. (There are, of course, exceptions to every rule.)

Focus on Women

When I hire a model, as opposed to booking through an agency, I always ask them to sign a standard stock-photography release, and I always pay them at the end of the day. That is only fair, even if the pictures don't sell for a year or more. It is also a good business practice, as my models are happy to work with me, willing to be available on short notice, and glad to go a little out of their way for me. In addition, when the pictures sell, I know that I don't have to check with the models. Occasionally, if a potential sale is for a particularly unusual use or client, I check back with the models to see if it is okay with them. And, very infrequently, I pay the models a little bonus if the photographs enjoy an especially big sale.

You can avoid a lot of problems by paying models on the spot and paying them well over the years. I speak from personal experience rather than a legal standpoint. The properly signed model release is

virtually airtight, but there is more to being a professional photographer and working with models than being sure that you have signed releases. I believe in treating people honestly and fairly, and doing so is ultimately to my benefit. I like and respect the people with whom I work. That is one of the reasons why I hire the same models again and again.

In this chapter, I discuss five models with whom I often work. Each one is a distinctly different type with a number of looks and strengths, depending on what the situation demands and how the shoot has been styled. One thing you'll probably notice is that, while these women are very attractive, none are outstandingly beautiful. They don't have the unusual, extreme looks of high-fashion models. Their beauty is believable, and they look like everyday women, perhaps dressed and made up for a big party or on a particularly good day.

Clean, Fresh, and Wholesome

Ten years ago, I was teaching a photography workshop in Asheville, North Carolina, and was interviewing models in New York City to take down with me. Molly came in for an interview because she was brand new to the business and needed pictures. She had an incredibly wholesome, "all-American" look, so I asked her to go to Asheville with me. I've been photographing her ever since—she never changes!

Two years ago, at my summer workshop in New York City, I was running a studio session on headshots that would be great for stock. Molly modeled for us against a white seamless-paper background. Two electronic-flash heads illuminated the paper from either side, and Molly was lit with a Mola light (see page 64) off to her left. After the students had taken their turns, I photographed a simple headshot of Molly (top right) using a very soft (#1) diffusion filter. I then photographed her without a filter, which proved to be quite profitable. One of the unfiltered headshots sold as a point-of-purchase counter card for a skin-care product. The client printed thousands of these cards and distributed them all around the country. You can see why this particular shot was chosen—it really shows off Molly's gorgeous skin. She looks clear, clean, and fresh.

The clown picture was also shot in my studio during a workshop. I set it up because Sharland, my assistant, really wanted to do clown makeup that day. I went along with the idea, although I had my reservations; I thought that it was the wrong type of picture for Molly and had no potential as stock. It certainly doesn't take advantage of Molly's remarkable skin, but it sold! Ilford, the photographic-supplies manufacturer, uses it at trade shows to demonstrate their photographic paper. I learned that, even with experience, it is difficult to predict what will sell. You can never really be certain which photographs will sell as stock and which won't. That uncertainty is part of the challenge, and excitement, of stock photography.

38

100% OIL FREE · DERMATOLOGIST TESTED

NEW!

Dramatic or Very Real

Phylis lives in Florida near my daughters, Jordana and Kendra. Whenever I visit them, I also spend at least half a day photographing Phylis for stock. My daughters usually suggest good locations nearby, and frequently, they come along and assist on shoots. All the pictures of Phylis shown on the next four pages were taken during two trips to Florida. The exception is the dramatic, orange-toned headshot (top right), which was photographed in my studio with tungsten lighting when Phylis came to visit me in New York.

Phylis is an absolutely ideal model for stock photography. She is quite versatile and flexible—perhaps not as "pigeon-holed" as some models. She moves beautifully and can convey many looks. She has a good dramatic sense, which is great for pictures with a fashion feel, and she can also appear "down-home" and genuine. All I have to do is provide Phylis with a storyline, and she puts herself right into it. She also brings her own clothes, and can do her own hair and makeup in a pinch (although I usually hire someone for this).

Phylis is slightly older than most models I photograph, and she is a brunette. Both characteristics are very saleable in stock photography today. Phylis's looks are not really what I would call ethnic, but she doesn't project the "all-American" look. Instead, with the right clothes, makeup, and setting, she can appear European, or perhaps even South American, which is wonderful for international stock sales.

On my first trip to Florida, I set up the picture of Phylis lying on the red car (bottom right) in my daughter Jordana's driveway. I was testing Fuji Velvia film, which is supposed to be great for colors, so we used an extremely bright dress, along with the purple hat and glasses. Phylis stretched out on the hood of the car, and I simply leaned out of Jordana's second-floor bedroom window. Fuji ended up buying this picture to advertise how well Velvia film records bright colors.

Dramatic or Very Real

On the second trip, I shot many photographs of Phylis at the Boca Raton Resort and Club, where my daughters are members. It is a fabulous location, the kind of place that normally demands official clearance and a location fee from photographers. Since we weren't actually shooting on assignment, the club management waived the fee and allowed us to wander all over the place. Perhaps one of the reasons the club didn't ask for a location fee (besides the fact that my daughters were members) was that we didn't cause a commotion. Although Phylis kept changing clothes, my daughters, Amy (the makeup artist), and I looked like a bunch of tourists taking snapshots. The club's public-relations lady even stopped by to say hello.

One of the pictures shot that day of Phylis in a white bathing suit, sitting by a pool (above), has sold as stock several times. *Family Circle* magazine ran the photograph across two pages (right). This picture is perfect for use in the health-and-fitness field (see chapter 4), and it might even work for a cosmetic company.

FAMILY CIRCLE • GREAT IDEAS

Still afraid to shed your winter coat? You know it's not as bad as all that.

Prepare to bare with a few extra exercises, some slimmer eating and the perfect swimsuit

42 FC FITNESS

COURTESY *FAMILY CIRCLE*

42

Mature and Energetic

Christine came to me when she started working with the modeling agency Gilla Roos. She needed a new portfolio and a *composite,* which is a promotional piece featuring a group of her best shots. Modeling agencies send out composites to solicit work. A good composite should always include a headshot and a full-length picture. I took one look at Christine and said, "You're an incredible type. I'll do a trade. You let me sell the pictures as stock, and I'll let you use the ones you like for your composite." It was a deal.

There is a giant market for stock photographs of attractive, energetic mature people. The magazine *Modern Maturity,* for example, has one of the largest circulations in the United States, if not the world. Think about demographics for a minute. Mature and retired people frequently have a lot of disposable income and the freedom to spend it; they

travel, and buy vacation homes and condominiums—they enjoy life! For some reason, advertisers never have enough quality pictures of healthy, energetic older people enjoying themselves. My stock agency is constantly asking me for such images, and my photographer friends tell me that their stock agencies need those types of pictures as well.

Christine is perfect for this market. She is spirited, attractive, and as vivacious as she looks. She is always full of ideas for photographs and willing to help out in any way she can. One day she brought her dog to my studio, and we used him in a series of shots. Another day, she suggested that we use Central Park for an outdoor shoot (below). Christine ended up creating her composite from my pictures alone, and I have no doubt that many of the same images will sell as stock.

Mature and Energetic

The only difference between shooting an older model like Christine and a young girl is that you have to imagine situations that would be appropriate for a mature woman. Everything else is the same, and the pictures can sell just as well, if not even better.

My stock agency had been asking for pictures of professional women, so I decided to photograph Christine as a doctor. I explained to her what I had in mind, and she pleasantly surprised me by borrowing a plaque from her own doctor's office and bringing it to the studio. We hung the plaque up in the corner of the studio where I have my lightbox, dressed Christine in a white coat and stethoscope that I keep as props, and she was perfect. The lighting for this picture was also easy: I used just one large umbrella in front of the set.

After we had finished taking all the pictures, Christine told me that she had been a model when she was younger, and that I had photographed her then, too. For some reason she hadn't wanted to tell me earlier. I thought back, and then I remembered working together over twenty years ago. I was amazed at how much time had passed and realized that a good model is probably a good model forever.

Spicy and Saucy

Leslie has a certain cocky, self-confident look that the camera just loves. There is something special about her eyes and about the way she holds herself when she is being photographed. Leslie is sexy, yet she doesn't look like a pinup model. She has a trimmer, tighter body than a centerfold type, making her an ideal model for sporting goods and fitness-oriented advertisements. She can play the part of someone who keeps in shape, and her little way of flirting with the camera puts just the right amount of spice in the picture.

All of these pictures of Leslie were taken for stock. The picture of her in a white business suit shows a more sophisticated side of Leslie. I used a very slight diffusion filter (#1) to add an element of romance.

The picture of Leslie with the male model James was taken at a country club in Connecticut. It is from a day-long shoot we did with several models (see page 30). Several pictures from that day have sold as stock, and this particular series led to a good assignment for a brand of ice tea.

Spicy and Saucy

A friend told me that a particular beach in New Jersey was a great location, so I decided to go there with Leslie and one assistant to do some test photographs of her in sporty bathing suits. When we arrived, the sky was totally overcast, and the beach was small and dirty, with almost no good settings or locations. All we'd brought in the way of clothing were the bathing suits and beach gear. I wished that I had packed my van full of different outfits, as I normally do, so that we could have taken other types of pictures. However, we decided to make the best of the situation. Leslie changed into her swimming gear, and we found one small lifeguard stand to work around. I deliberately threw the background out of focus.

To my surprise, once we started shooting, the energy flowed. It turned out that the soft, overcast light made the bathing suit's colors pop out against the background, and the light also flattered Leslie's face and skin. I think the pictures we took in that gray, horrible place actually came out quite well. There is a lesson to be learned here: With a little flexibility, the right attitude, and the right people, you can turn a potentially disastrous shoot into a true success.

Young and Gifted

I met Kim while giving a short workshop at Cypress Gardens in Florida to a local photographers' group. The group had arranged with an agency in Orlando to provide models for my demonstrations. One of the girls the agency sent was Kim.

She was very young at the time (she is still less than twenty years old), and the workshop was incredibly hectic, but after only a few minutes it became clear that this girl was good. Not only was she beautiful, with fantastic skin, but she knew just how to move and pose almost automatically. With barely any experience, she was better than some models are after five years in the business. It is fair to say that Kim has photographic modeling in her blood.

During a break on that crazy day, Kim told me that she was really new in the business. She asked if I would work with her to build up her portfolio if she came to New York. I said yes, and invited her to come to the city and stay with me.

Kim came to New York to model in a week-long workshop at my studio, and all of the pictures shown here were taken then. She was even better than I had thought she would be. Besides being a great model, she was full of ideas and bursting with enthusiasm. Once, she went into the dressing room to change between shots, and the next thing I knew, she returned with a black tutu on her head and said, "Isn't this great?" It was great, so we worked on her makeup, picked out some appropriate earrings,

put her on the set, and I took photos of her wearing the tutu like a wig (below). The pictures were fantastic, and we had great fun.

The shot of Kim with the seashell was less spontaneous, but it also came out very well and sold as stock to *Victoria* magazine. This picture really shows off Kim's fantastic skin. I can't overemphasize the importance of skin in a female model. I may be a bit of a nut on the subject, but I always look carefully at a woman's skin if I'm considering photographing her. I'll always choose a model with better skin over one with more striking features. You can't hide less-than-perfect skin—not with lighting, filters, or even retouching. Skin quality always shows through, and I find that it makes or breaks a photograph.

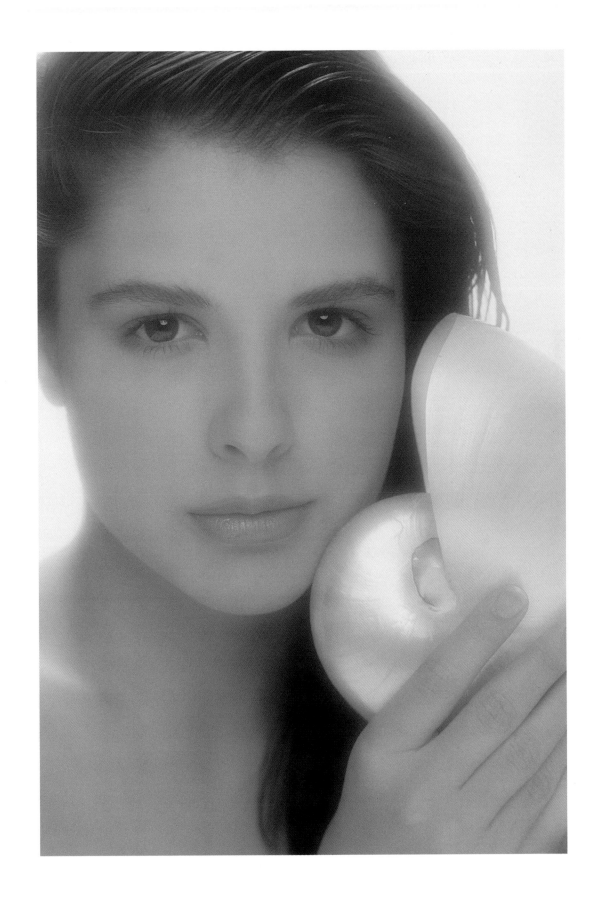

Young and Gifted

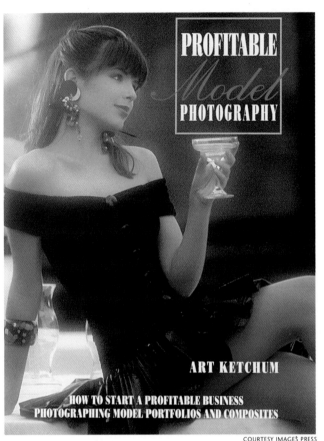

COURTESY IMAGES PRESS

This diagram shows the set, shot at night on the roof of my building. Colored gels were put on the flash heads to create a festive atmosphere. A low-power flash head, or kicker, *was used to fill in light from a low angle.*

FLASH HEADS COVERED WITH COLORED GELS

KICKER

FLASH HEAD POINTING INTO UMBRELLA ON BOOM

CAMERA

The story behind the picture of Kim holding a glass of champagne (far left) illustrates her lively character. During every workshop I run in New York, we do one outdoor shoot at night. During the week of Kim's visit, the class suggested doing the night shoot on the roof of the building where I have my studio, so we set up a "party" situation. Electronic-flash heads covered with orange gel added atmosphere to the background. We rigged the flash heads to use photo cells so they would fire at the same time as the main light source: a flash and a large umbrella. This setup illuminated the table and the foreground. Long exposures captured the skyline and created a sense of movement.

Kim immediately started working with the feeling and mood. She picked up a glass of imitation champagne and started flirting with a male model. I looked at the glass and said, "Kim, you're too young to drink." "No," she said. "I'm at a party, and I'm having a good time." She is a real actress, and part of her charm is that she jumps into the spirit of a situation.

This "champagne" picture sold quickly as the cover for a book on modeling. The publisher's photo researcher came to my studio one day and started looking through my files. She'd only gone through part of one drawer when she came across the picture of Kim. She selected it even though the original is a horizontal and the book format was vertical. I guess it was obvious that Kim is a natural model.

Simple Headshots

Few photographers realize that there is an enormous market for simple stock photographs of the face. Portraits are the most basic and classic photographic images. A good, clean picture of the face somehow captures or conveys personality unlike any other picture. Simple shots of faces are used on everything from national advertisements and product coupons to magazine articles about cosmetics and the covers of bestselling mystery novels.

Stock-photography clients are always looking for fresh, new faces. I've kept an eye out for interesting headshots ever since a major international company used a group of my portraits on the cover of their annual report. The company wanted the cover to reflect the fact that they had branches in many different countries, so they decided to feature faces representing ethnic groups from around the world. They had a devil of a time finding simple headshots of attractive people. Not enough photographers have anticipated the need for those types of pictures, and back then, not many stock-photo agencies had them in their files. In the end, practically all the pictures used on the cover were mine, supplied by The Image Bank.

In the excitement of casting, locating props, finding unusual locations, setting up intriguing storylines, and creating interesting lifestyle or fashion situations, many photographers neglect to take headshots of their models. I make it a point to take headshots of every person I photograph, both on location and in the studio. I usually prepare a simple, smaller set in the studio right next to the main set for this purpose. On location, I make sure that I often come in close and concentrate on the models' faces.

Simple Headshots

When I speak of *headshots,* I mean closeup, tightly cropped pictures of faces. Many photographers refer to headshots with slightly deprecating overtones. Nonetheless, it is the term used in the modeling industry, and, having been a model for many years and worked with models for even longer, I am comfortable with it. The type of headshots I usually take, particularly the ones shown in this chapter, are known as *beauty photographs.* A lot of beauty photographs are, in fact, sold to cosmetic companies. These pictures

are quite clean and professional, and the models are carefully made up, but I don't consider beauty shots particularly special or tough to do. Often, they are simply outtakes from a much larger shoot, which is another reason I distinguish them as headshots.

The tearsheets on these two pages show just a fraction of the ways my headshots have sold as stock. The Image Bank keeps track of all my sales; often, I have no idea how and when my pictures will appear. Once your photographs enter the international stock

marketplace, you lose virtually any say in where and how they are used. Logistics dictate that the possibility of your seeing (or receiving) copies of each usage is very small, which is why obtaining signed releases from models and property owners when you shoot is so important. Before putting your photographs into the world market as stock, you must decide whether you are legally protected or can live with the consequences if you are not.

The dramatic shot of Victoria on the cover of *Marketing Communications* magazine is an

COURTESY AVON BOOKS

example of a picture that sold without my knowledge. I spotted it at a newsstand by accident and bought a copy. I was surprised that this particular picture had sold because Victoria's earrings are almost too prominent. Jewelry and accessories should lend something to a photograph, but in order to maximize sales, they shouldn't stand out too much. Jewelry can also date a picture—be sure to use classic, timeless pieces whenever possible. Remember, it is your job to draw the fine line between style and what the market will bear.

SAVE $1.00

Scented

lady speed stick
ANTI-PERSPIRANT
by MENNEN

DE SOLID

*And Win
A Day of Beauty
From* lady speed stick

COURTESY HELLER & COHEN

CARING FOR THE WOMAN IN MOM

COMPLIMENTS OF *Stayfree*

COURTESY THE GUILD GROUP

59

Enhancing Natural Beauty

This is one of my favorite photographs. The model, Jodyann, has stunning red hair, but I'm most amazed by her beautiful blue eyes. I sometimes wonder if she is wearing special contact lenses to enhance their color. Her eyes are so unusually blue that they could seem almost frightening.

This photograph was taken during one of the workshops at my New York studio a few summers ago. Whenever I give a workshop, I take advantage of the opportunity to shoot photographs for stock. The situation is ideal: My students learn by watching me do real work, rather than a simple demonstration, that they then duplicate, and I

certainly don't mind making double use of my time. Afterward, they compare their ideas and photographs with mine.

I wanted to show the class how to use colored gels with electronic-flash lighting, and Jodyann's stunning red hair presented a perfect opportunity: We would make her hair even redder. To do so, we

placed a red gel and a grid spot over a flash head and positioned it above and slightly behind the model. The flash highlighted the edges of Jodyann's hair, thus separating it from the black-velvet background. The red gel over the flash made those highlights red, rather than white, their normal color. Because the flash was behind Jodyann, it didn't influence her skin color. We used reddish-pink lipstick and chose a hot-pink blouse and earrings in order to harmonize all of the colors in the picture. Coordinating a picture's colors makes it more marketable.

It didn't take long for this picture to sell as stock. A few days after the workshop was over, a cosmetic company called to see my portfolio. I sent it to them including the headshot from the workshop. They took one look at the picture and said, "This would be perfect for a lipstick counter card." We negotiated a price, and I sold them the right to use this image on counter cards in the United States for one year.

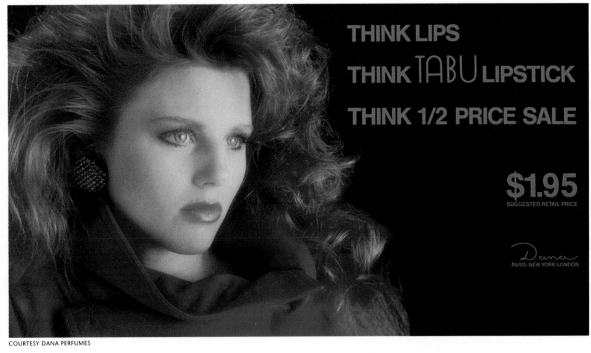

COURTESY DANA PERFUMES

A silver reflector was positioned under Jodyann's face. The flash head directly over her included a grid spot for diffusion. The Chimera banklight, positioned 45 degrees to Jodyann's left, was placed on its side at a level higher than the model.

Model Releases: A Lesson Learned

I learned the hard way why it is important to get signed model releases at the time of a shoot. A model came to my studio one day and said she wanted to do some testing. I had a few ideas for photographs I wanted to try out, so I agreed and we set up a date. The shoot went quite well, but for some reason I can't remember, I didn't have her sign a release. Still, I was happy with the headshot of her in fur with falling "snow" (below left), and I added it to my portfolio. Later, the same client who bought the picture of the redhead on page 60 also wanted to buy the rights to this picture. I told the cosmetic company that there was no model release, but if they got in touch with the model's agency and paid a fee, there should be no problem. I even gave them the model's name and the number of her agency.

There was a problem. The agency wanted a very large fee for the rights to use the photograph. It was a ridiculous amount, especially considering that the picture had already been shot and no more model time was needed. Negotiations ensued, but the agency wouldn't budge. The client called me with this news and said, unfortunately, that they wouldn't be able to use my photograph.

Then I made an unusual suggestion: I offered to reshoot the picture with another model. I told the client, "You don't have to make any promises. I'll reshoot it, and if you like the picture when it is finished, you can buy it." The client agreed and suggested that I use a blonde model.

I was pretty sure that the picture would sell as stock, even if that client didn't buy it, so I called up another model, Daryl Meyer. I explained that I was doing the shoot "on spec," or on speculation. If the client bought the picture, Daryl would get an additional fee. If not, she would have a good picture for her portfolio, and I would put the pictures into stock. She agreed to sign a release for the shoot.

In the end, the client bought the rights to the second picture (opposite, right), and Daryl received an additional fee from the client. I haven't seen the first model since, but someday I will run into her.

When I do, I'll probably tell her how unreasonable her agency was and how they lost her a client who was more than willing to pay.

An explanation is in order regarding the "snow" used in both versions of the picture. I have two kinds of fake snow in the studio: big snowflakes and little snowflakes. The big flakes are good for sets but don't look real up close. Little flakes are more realistic and better looking for headshots. To photograph snow "falling," I have an assistant stand on the side and shake the little flakes down onto the set from a colander. Afterward, we use an empty vacuum cleaner to pick it all up and store it for the next use.

COURTESY DANA PERFUMES

Color, Color, Color

Fuji Film had given me a number of rolls of Fujichrome Velvia to test. They said this color-transparency film produced great color and extremely sharp images. I decided to use the Velvia for a carefully planned series of stock photographs designed to highlight bright colors. To take full advantage of the film's sharpness, I hired Jean Severs, an excellent model with wonderful skin, for the shoot.

When Jean came in for the shoot, I had everything set up for headshots. Jean sat with her elbows propped up on a small, adjustable table that I use for portrait work. I placed a single Mola light right in front of her. You can see the reflection of the round Mola light in her eyes (right).

A Mola light is a round, metal banklight coated inside with a special white reflecting paint; it can be adapted to any flash head. A Mola light gives a very even, soft, wraparound light. It features a diffusion filter that can be removed for a slightly harder light, but I generally leave the filter on it. Mola lights come in two diameters: 3 feet and 18 inches. I have two large ones and one small one. The small Mola works very well above a subject's head or very close up front. I keep Mola lights on booms in the studio, and I use them more than any other lights.

They never leave the studio. I particularly like to use the small Mola in front of the subject when I'm working with an 80-200mm zoom lens. This permits me to get up close and frame the picture tightly without having to crawl underneath the light (the longer focal-length setting on the lens permits me to work from farther back and in more comfort).

Color, Color, Color

After finishing the pictures intended for stock, I decided to try an experiment (right) using brightly colored gloves and hats. I arranged these colorful props around Jean's face and came in really tight. I'd used the brightly colored gloves for years; I love the way they look, and they stretch to almost any size (kids as well as grownups can wear them). The best kind of prop you can own is one that works for many situations. The hat in the picture is actually two hats: a red one underneath a purple one, with the red one rolled up to show.

When I showed Fuji the pictures as part of the deal for using their film, they immediately asked to use the "experimental one" on the cover of a brochure (right). This not only showed how well the Velvia reproduced bright colors but also how extremely sharp her skin appeared. The only drawback to the film was that Jean's skin came out slightly warmer than it was in real life.

Fuji used the picture almost exactly as I photographed it (far right), and, as a matter of fact, the art director complained about how tight the cropping was. It didn't leave him much room to play with around the edges. Coming in too close to the subject can be a costly mistake when you're shooting for stock. Be sure to leave a little extra room in your pictures so that they can be cropped for a specific format.

COURTESY FUJI PHOTO FILM USA, INC.

Health and Fitness Are Hot

Everyone in America knows that the health and fitness market is booming. It seems as if another health club opens up every week in my neighborhood, and every month a new sport or exercise machine becomes the latest fad. Images of good health are considered very sexy right now and are used to sell many products that aren't remotely connected to healthy living. The market for health and fitness stock photographs is enormous, and, as luck would have it, these subjects fit right into in my own upbeat style.

The sports-oriented photograph of the man on the left is, I think you'll agree, a great stock picture. The model is attractive, and his expression is fantastic. The lighting is strong, and the colors in the picture work well together. In my experience, however, what really helps sell this picture as stock is that no brand names appear anywhere. If you look closely at the volleyball, you'll notice that my assistants disguised its brand name with colored marker pens.

Except for a brand's manufacturer, potential clients worry about legal issues if a brand name appears prominently in a picture. Or perhaps the picture wouldn't be appropriate in geographic areas where that brand is unavailable or out of season. Also, from a more emotional standpoint, clients are going to wonder why they should spend money to help advertise or promote another company's product.

Labels can be retouched out of a picture, but to a picture buyer, it makes more sense to choose an image that doesn't need retouching. Not including brand names in photographs underscores one of my basic rules of thumb—for a picture to be really successful in the international stock-photo market, it shouldn't be too closely associated with any specific time or place.

Health and Fitness Are Hot

Closely related to the fitness concept, but a little less obvious, is the market for "Health" photographs with a capital *H*—photographs that can be used to advertise pharmaceutical and medical health products. This extremely lucrative market generates a lot of income for certain stock photographers. One reason that stock shot for pharmaceutical and medical advertising earns top dollars is that there is so much money at stake for the manufacturers. They spend years and millions of dollars developing new drugs, and once

they've perfected them and received approval from the various regulatory agencies, they don't skimp on their advertising and promotion.

Another reason pharmaceutical and medical stock is so lucrative for professional shooters is that it falls into an area referred to in commercial photography as "sensitive subjects." For obvious reasons, not all models are willing to allow their faces to be associated with disease or a treatment for a medical disorder. As a result, pharmaceutical advertisers frequently pay a premium for the photographs

they use, as well as an additional fee to the model.

When my stock-photo agency intends to license one of my photographs for a pharmaceutical advertisement, someone at the agency always calls me to verify that the model releases are in order. Before I fax a copy of my releases to the agency, I find out as much as I can about the product to be advertised and how the photographs will be used. If I have any doubts, I call and check with the models in question. This is only fair and honest. I don't want the models

whom I photograph to see their faces used in a way they might personally regret. Keep in mind that your word-of-mouth reputation among your colleagues plays an important role in developing a successful photography business.

Most of the pictures shown in this chapter are aimed more at the general and consumer fitness market than at the pharmaceutical market. A number of them, however, could be used either way, and the two nudes on pages 76-77 were shot specifically for the pharmaceutical and medical market.

Spa Appeal

A major magazine called one day and asked me to do a shoot the next morning for an article on health spas. They wanted an artistic picture, an impressionistic approach that conveyed the concept and feeling of health spas in general, rather than any specific aspect of them. I came up with an idea, discussed it on the phone with the magazine, and was given the go-ahead. My studio staff jumped into production at full speed.

The next day the magazine called again and said they'd decided against doing the photograph. I can't remember what reason they used to cancel, but I had all my lighting set up, a painted backdrop rented and in the studio, and a model and hair-and-makeup person standing by. Since everything was ready to go, I said to my staff, "So what if the client canceled. Let's do the shoot anyway. I'll put the pictures into stock."

These are some of the pictures I took that day. As you can see, I photographed the situation first with conventional slide film (above), and then with high-speed slide film for increased grain (below). While the straight picture is actually quite beautiful, the grainy one has a more artistic or impressionistic feeling. The grain helps move the image one step further away from reality, and closer to a dream or fantasy.

I used to use a complicated, multi-filter technique (there were about four filters in the pack) and

special film processing to achieve a grainy look. Today, I just use Agfachrome 1000 film, rated at ISO 1000. Granted, I still have the film processed specially, using clip tests to see which development time produces pure whites, but not having to use all those filters makes my life much easier. I sincerely believe in making photographic technique as simple as possible. Without undue complications, I can concentrate on what really matters—what is going on in front of me and the images I am capturing with the camera.

You might wonder whether the magazine that originally asked me to shoot these pictures paid me a cancellation fee. After all, I had gone to the time and expense of getting everything ready at the magazine's request. Well, they didn't pay me anything. Many professional photographers would, justifiably, have asked for something for their, and their staff's, time and work. But this was an editorial job, and magazines generally don't have budgets for such contingencies. Knowing this, I just made the best of the situation and tried to turn it to my advantage.

Also, I am quite certain these pictures will sell well as stock. They might even sell for a little more than average stock photos, because they are slightly more artistic. That is my hope; in fact, one of the few changes I'd really like to see in stock photography is higher fees paid for higher quality. Even though a stock-photo fee is based on how the picture is used and how many people are going to see it, I think some allowance should be made for the quality of the picture. A picture that is more artistic, or that was much more difficult to produce, should sell for a slightly higher price than a simpler picture. I believe this idea is catching on.

Spa Appeal

Here is another stylized, idealized interpretation of the concept and feeling of health spas. The pictures on the right are perhaps more directly related to a specific aspect of spas—saunas—than those on the last four pages, yet they still have an interpretive, impressionistic quality. They are ideal stock images for several reasons: You can't see the models' faces (remember— photograph people from behind whenever it works for the situation); there are no obvious brand names (even the patterns on the colored towels aren't tied to any particular country or manufacturer); and the white towels are about as classic as you can get. The fact that these pictures convey a great deal of feeling and mood, while remaining nonspecific in terms of subject,

means they will probably sell quite well as stock. This shoot took a lot of work, but its sales over the next few years should prove that it was worth it!

The key element in shooting these pictures was a very large (approximately 4 × 8 feet) piece of pebbled Plexiglas, the kind that many people associate with shower stalls. As you can see in the production photograph (below), we suspended the Plexiglas between two extendible support rods and put it between the models and the camera. The texture of the Plexiglas, and the way it distorted or abstracted the models, is what makes these pictures work. Without the Plexiglas, these pictures would probably be quite boring.

The tricky part was the lighting, and it took us quite a while to get it just right. Whenever you photograph through Plexiglas, glass, plastic, or anything translucent, you really have to watch out for reflections. Quite often, your lights will hit these surfaces at an angle that causes them to reflect back at the camera, producing glare. When the angle is totally wrong, you photograph nothing but glare. With an angle that is just slightly off, you produce washed-out colors and perhaps little six-sided spots, which also occur when the sun hits your lens.

The simplest solution to the reflection problem is to put all lights on the far side of the glass. On our shoot, however, we wanted the Plexiglas to show texture, which meant that the lights had to strike the front of the surface, preferably at a hard angle. Our solution was to put a very large, even light source on the side of the set. To make this work, we stretched a large sheet of translucent white parachute nylon in front of a number of electronic-flash heads. This light source then lit both the front of the Plexiglas and the models behind it. If you look very carefully at the resulting pictures, you can see that we should have used an even larger light source, as there is some fall-off in the light on the far side.

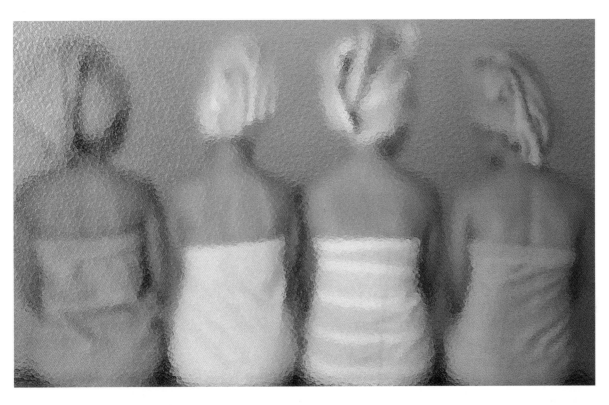

Strictly Anatomy

Unlike the other photographs in this chapter, these two nudes were created specifically for the pharmaceutical and medical advertising market, as opposed to the more general health field. The picture of the nude veiled with the translucent cloth could perhaps be used to advertise a beauty or skin product. The other image is of a human body, pure and simple. It is not stylized or romanticized, and though the model has a good body, it is not a particularly erotic pose. She is just standing there, very real and natural.

Both pictures were shot in my studio during a whole day's worth of shooting stock photographs. We used the simplest of white backgrounds so there would be no sense of time or place. In the picture of the curtained nude (far right), we used a large, soft light source for extremely flat illumination. In the simple nude picture (right), we used harder light (and oiled the model) in order to really focus on skin and form. I kept the model's face out of the pictures on purpose. She is a consummate professional as a model, so I'm not sure she would have had a problem if her face showed, but there are some things it is better not to do.

The Sporting Life

This shoot demonstrates the importance of recognizing opportunity when it knocks, and then taking advantage of it to create great stock photographs at a reasonable cost. I had photographed Christy, the female model in these pictures, many times and knew she was a very good model. One day she called and said she had cut her beautiful blonde hair quite short. She had a brand-new, healthy look and needed a whole set of new pictures to show it. She also knew a good male model, Chris, who needed new pictures, and she suggested we all go to Jamaica for five days of photography. We would each pay our own way. She and Chris could use the photos for their portfolios, and I could sell them as stock. I agreed almost instantly.

It was off-season, so we found very reasonable rates for the airfare and for a hotel suite designed for four people. I brought an assistant, along with cameras, lots of film, flex-fill reflectors (flexible reflectors for filling in light), and a battery-powered flash unit. We also took a huge bag jammed with swimsuits, fins, snorkels and masks, bright towels, hats, sunglasses, inflatable rafts, a number of dresses in a rainbow of colors, and much more. I didn't want to waste any time searching for clothing and props once we arrived in Jamaica.

The Sporting Life

All the locations we needed were near each other, and the one we used the most was the beach right behind the hotel. The weather was wonderful, so we only photographed in the early mornings and late afternoons, when the light was at its best, and quit during the middle of each day.

All the pictures were taken with available light (that tropical sun is great!), and as usual I covered every situation in depth, shooting both horizontals and verticals, coming in close and moving farther back. I shot some situations with both regular film and high-speed film (for a grainy look), and I had the models change clothes at least once during each shoot. Since the whole idea was to present a natural, casual look, Christy did her own makeup, and we just let her short hair do what it would.

Christy's short hair had an athletic, healthy look, so we did several scenarios on that theme, for example, riding horses, snorkeling, and so on. However, I also worked with the exotic and sensual mood of the setting, and took many pictures of Christy and Chris as a "romantic couple." Christy and Chris worked together beautifully, and their looks complement each other. They readily picked up on the sultry, sensuous atmosphere of Jamaica and conveyed something of the same mood in their poses and actions. The lush tropical foliage and the clear water worked perfectly as backgrounds that say "tropical island" but are not recognizable as any specific island or country.

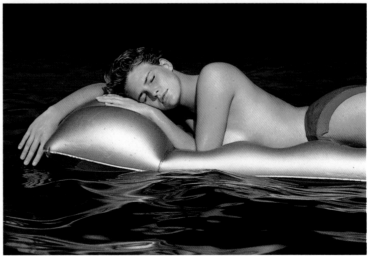

A funny thing happened on the next-to-last day of the shoot. The manager of the hotel came up to me and said that one of the guests wanted me to photograph her. She didn't ask herself for fear that she would disturb us. The guest turned out to be a beautiful black woman whom we had all noticed. She was stunning, and she was always dressed remarkably. Her name was Jewel, and it turned out that she was a model from New York on vacation. She had even been in my studio once on a casting call.

I said I would be glad to photograph her, and picked up a white one-piece bathing suit and a yellow bikini in the hotel's gift shop. They worked beautifully on her. She has an excellent figure and turned out to be a very professional model. Since then, I've even hired her for jobs and stock shoots in New York.

May to December, Couples Sell

Couples have always been a mainstay of the stock business. There are couples for every stage of life, from young lovers to newlyweds, parents to grandparents. Each type of couple is a great stock subject because clients are always trying to sell something to people in these categories. In fact, you could make your living just shooting couples for stock. Most locations are perfect for them; for example, a beach at sunset is ready-made for any couple. Clients never tire of this motif because pictures of happy couples encourage people to buy the clients' products. Viewers look at these photographs and wish that they were part of the fun. Such pictures sell quite well as stock and always will.

Because a market exists for pictures of many different kinds of couples, you don't have to specialize in photographing young honeymooners or teenagers on a date. At the same time, the shooting situations you design for your couples—what they do, as well as their props and clothing—should be appropriate for the type and age of the models you are using. You wouldn't show senior citizens carrying skateboards, obviously. By the same token, I wouldn't suggest photographing a very young couple in an elegant and expensive café. A diner, or a hotdog stand by the beach, would be much more appropriate.

The situations and settings you devise for couple shoots don't always have to be as romantic as a moonlit beach. Clients are often looking for a sense of reality, the kind of setting that their customers can associate with and believe. It is true that romance is where you find it, and much of the world finds romance in more common locations. In the context of photography, romance only exists when and where you and your models make it happen.

May to December, Couples Sell

Directing two models to interact affectionately is crucial to creating the illusion of romance. If they stand stiffly side by side, your pictures are going to resemble formal high-school prom portraits or pictures of an awkward first date. Not all models are good at interacting as couples. Working closely with members of the opposite sex who aren't their real-life lovers, yet appearing relaxed, affectionate, and comfortable, can be a tall order for some people. Knowing which models work well in couple situations, and which models don't, is one of the advantages of working repeatedly with the same people.

In general, tell your models to laugh and touch, look at and speak to each other, rather than to the camera; however, this isn't a hard-and-fast rule. Sometimes a little eye contact with the lens really makes an image click. One trick for inspiring natural-looking expressions is to tell your models at the beginning of a shoot not to look at you unless explicitly asked. Then, yelling "look at me!" quite suddenly can produce some great expressions.

Be careful not to overshoot a situation, as this will dampen any enthusiasm and liveliness in both you and the models. For me, overshooting isn't necessarily related to the amount of film used. The number of frames you shoot should only depend on how well *you* feel the situation is going.

When you are certain that you've made good pictures and covered the situation completely, you can stop shooting. Better yet, once you know you've shot some great photographs, shoot a few more rolls; then stop.

I always bring more film on location than I think I'll need, and I shoot most of it. Perhaps the only thing more frustrating than running out of film when things are going great is having the batteries in your camera die. (That is why I always bring along extra camera batteries, and I'm an expert at changing them extremely fast.) Also, running out of film doesn't make financial sense. Having gone to the expense and effort of setting up a good shoot, you want to make pictures that will sell well enough to do more than just recoup your expenses. You need to make a profit from your effort and talent. Bestselling pictures don't automatically come at the beginning of a shoot, so if you can possibly afford it, don't skimp on film.

This chapter features photographs of four kinds of couples: a group of young friends in their early twenties who aren't quite paired off yet; a middle-aged couple who could be parents on vacation; a European couple; and finally, a retired couple still very much in love. You'll see how the differences in their dress, situations, and activities convey unique messages to viewers.

Young Friends or Lovers?

These pictures were taken on a shoot in the resort town of Spring Lake, New Jersey. The storyline that day was simply "young couples having fun." Bright colors were used to emphasize the sense of fun. I also wanted a very commercial feeling. I'd been shooting a lot of beauty pictures in very pale tones for a few weeks, and I needed some energy and color in my work.

When I visualized the shoot, I had certain models in mind—J.D., Jean, and Michael, whom I've used many times. I knew that they could do exactly what I wanted. I called my Connecticut agent, Ester Johnston, and booked them. I also asked Michael to bring his car, for which I paid an additional fee.

We worked out of a room in a bed and breakfast that I had rented for the day. On shoots of this type, I generally use off-season vacation destinations. Prices are lower, and there aren't large crowds of vacationers in your way. You frequently have the run of the place for yourself and your crew.

I planned to photograph the three models as couples and as singles. I had instructed them to look at me with big smiles so that the viewer could feel their energy. I usually don't go after such specific

88

images, but I wanted a certain mood and carefully selected every detail.

I wanted a very active, energetic feeling in almost all the photographs because that was appropriate for the age and look of the models. We had a volleyball and lots of other sports equipment to use for props, and I'd brought plenty of brightly colored clothing from New York. I had the models interact with me a lot because it seemed to give the pictures more energy.

We shot the whole day, changing the situations and locations as the light progressed. I switched the pairings frequently, sometimes retaking the same picture with two different couples. That way, if a potential client somewhere in the world doesn't like the look of one of the men, there is another option.

All three models were great. They energetically put themselves right into the activities, and really moved and worked. I mean physically *worked*; everyone was very tired when the day was over but also happy, with the feeling of a job well done. It was the best kind of shoot a stock photographer can do.

Note the cropping in the picture with the car (far left). I framed the image very tightly to eliminate details of the car's make, model, and year. You can still tell that the car is a convertible, but no specific time or place is implied. This makes the picture saleable in more markets, increases its appeal to more clients, and prevents it from dating quickly.

Grownup Pleasures

This older, more middle-aged couple was photographed in Clearwater, Florida. I was visiting my daughter Kendra and did a half-day shoot on the beach. I'd been shooting very young couples and retired people quite a bit, and needed to take some pictures of the in-between look. I found the two models, John and Janis, through an Orlando modeling agency that I'd used before. The concept behind these pictures was an intimate "weekend away." Perhaps this couple are parents on a short vacation from the responsibilities of children, jobs, and home; or, they could be unmarried but romantically involved.

As you can see, the scenarios I created for this couple are much less strenuous than those I used for the younger models. The reason is that middle-aged people have different ways of relaxing—they don't normally carry people around, ride on the top of a convertible's back seat, or play beach volleyball hard and fast.

To show older models doing such things would make the pictures less than believable. Remember, the goal of a stock-photography shoot is to make the situation and pictures appear as real as possible (unless you're trying to create a feeling of fantasy).

I made this couple look active, energetic, and involved, but instead of showing the man hoisting the woman above the waves, I photographed them relaxing in the wash of the surf (below). In real life, they probably wouldn't go out for a night of dancing and carousing, so I posed the models as if they were romantically sharing a quiet drink on the balcony of their hotel room, perhaps before going out for a good dinner (left).

The pictures of both generations of couples convey the same messages of energy and interaction. The only real difference is that the activities in which each couple is engaged are appropriate for their ages. The changes in their activities are simply a matter of degree.

Love, European–Style

This couple, Arik and Taryn, were photographed specifically for the European market. The models certainly don't look "all-American," and the settings have a distinctly "old city" quality. Arik is Israeli, but he looks French, and so does Taryn. Most of the pictures from this series were taken outdoors in the Greenwich Village neighborhood of New York City, which has a European flavor. Notice that the settings I chose have walls with peeling paint (rather than perfect surfaces), and the colors are much less bright and vibrant than many of the other photographs in this book. All the pictures have a "snapshot" quality to them, especially the one with Taryn looking down (above). You can only see part of her face.

The picture of Arik and Taryn at a café (top, far right) was actually taken in the studio. I intended to shoot the café scene in the Village after the street scene, but it was winter and very cold outside, and the sun set very early. However, I had planned ahead. The night before, I'd rented a painted backdrop from Charles Broderson, set it up, and had it lit. (There are many sources for painted backgrounds in New York and other large cities. Most suppliers can provide you with a catalog of their offerings.) The backdrop resembled a wall that had been painted too many

times and stained by age, much like the buildings in Greenwich Village. It certainly didn't look clean and pristine.

We put orange gels on the flash heads to give the photographs a sunset, outdoor feeling. The photograph of the whole set (right) shows where the lights were. Using a zoom lens, I stayed far away from the models, so I could shoot the full café and come in tight. The Image Bank loved Arik and has since asked me to do more with him. He is a good ethnic type and a very natural model.

Golden Romance

Here we have another couple, much older but still very much in love. They are grandparents and could be retired, but they continue to be active: painting, fishing, and enjoying the beauties of nature. Most important, they share these activities as a couple. The models are my friends from Connecticut, the Chitwoods, seen earlier on page 32. The Image Bank is always asking for new pictures of mature, active people, and for pictures of family situations with grandparents,

so I do shoots with the Chitwoods several times a year.

The photographs shown here were made during two different shoots, one in late summer and one in autumn. The clothing and props belong to the Chitwoods, and they found and suggested all the locations. The backyard is their own, the park and the beautiful, tree-lined street are in their home town only a few minutes from their house, and the beach is down at the end of the street on which they live.

For both of these shoots I drove my van from New York City to Connecticut, carrying just my camera case, and met the Chitwoods. Then we drove from location to location in their car. Their daughter even assisted at one of the shoots, holding a reflector when it was needed. You can't expect much more cooperation and assistance from models than that.

The Chitwoods' activities are appropriately sedate for their age

but still reflect an active lifestyle. These photographs really captured the interaction and affection between them, especially the picture of the two of them huddled together on a park bench on a chilly but sunny fall day (right). Of course, the Chitwoods are married and still very much in love. That certainly made it easier to create a picture that conveys this feeling than it would be working with two models who are essentially strangers.

Golden Romance

The picture of the Chitwoods standing together on a bridge (left) has many advantages in terms of stock photography. First, it shows only their backs, not their faces. Their anonymity makes the picture saleable in many markets because you aren't certain how old they are or what their nationality is. Viewers can use their imagination and project whatever personality or origin they wish onto these figures. Whenever possible, remember to photograph your models from the back and in silhouette. Pictures of anonymous models sell very well and often.

This photograph also contains plenty of room for type. There is the solid water area and the shadow under the bridge; even the trees, which are on the dark side, are solid enough in tone to allow an overlay of type. There could be a little more room across the top of the picture for the name of a magazine, but then the photograph wouldn't include a complete reflection of the couple. I opted to frame the image for the whole reflection rather than leave more room at the top.

Another selling point for the bridge picture, as well as the closeup of the Chitwoods (below), is that they are the focal point because they are dressed primarily in red. Bright colors draw the viewer's attention, and no color stands out like red. The fact that the clothing is classically styled, rather than being particularly of-the-moment or fashionable, should help the picture sell in many areas of the world and for years to come.

Stock Agency Requests

To sell a lot of stock photographs, you have to produce images that fit potential clients' needs. Your stock agency is the best source for learning what the market demands. All the photographs discussed in this chapter were based on very specific requests from my agency. Your agency should constantly send you lists of "requested subjects." Don't ignore them if you are serious about being a professional and making money in stock photography.

Stock agencies send out request lists of subjects that are needed for their files: subjects frequently in demand and those missing entirely. The agency might also ask for pictures of a subject projected to be in demand in the future. Or a request list might even reflect subjects in which an agency specializes, but with a need for new material. Seeing old material in an agency's file really turns off potential clients.

The editors and salespeople at a stock agency are good sources of picture ideas. They can suggest props, clothing, and hair styles that will increase the overseas-sales potential for your pictures. They know what types of requests are coming in and where they are losing sales because of gaps in their files. By shooting to fill holes in their files, you will help your agency and increase the probability of sales for your pictures. In my experience, working closely with an agency has great benefits.

Sometimes it takes discipline to shoot photographs for agency request lists. You may think their ideas are boring, or clichéd, or corny, but if you don't study those lists, your income from stock photography will suffer. Whatever reason a subject appears on your stock agency's list, you can be sure that photographs of that subject will sell. It simply makes sense to shoot with those sales in mind.

Stock Agency Requests

Don't try to shoot everything that an agency wants; you physically can't do it. Just shoot what you can do well and would love to photograph anyway. I'm not about to shoot mountains in Peru, because I like to photograph people. There are plenty of requests by agencies for people shots, and when they call for those, I listen.

You have to discipline yourself to do stock-agency requests because they are often of subjects you aren't dying to do. I shot some of the pictures in this book for myself, but many more were done at my agency's request. However, when the shooting starts, I always enjoy myself, whether I'm working on a self-assignment or to fulfill a request. I have fun with my models and the situations, and I make the most of them. For example, I can't say I'm thrilled to photograph guys in business suits on Wall Street, but once we begin the shoot, and the models are running around with their ties flying (bottom right), we all warm up to the idea, and the shoot becomes exciting. I can shoot my favorite subjects until I'm blue in the face, but if I don't take the time to go through The Image Bank's request lists to understand its needs—and shoot stock with those lists in mind—I'm just not in business as a stock photographer.

My theory about stock photography is that you should concentrate in a few areas to be really successful and to do the best work. A friend who works for a stock agency told me about a photographer who shoots nothing but trucks—all kinds of trucks. He does it because he loves trucks and knows them well. He makes a very good living from his specialty. I would never try to fill a stock agency's request for pictures of trucks (unless they wanted models with trucks). What I photograph is people, which is why I'm successful in stock photography: I shoot what I love, in my own style, with an eye for what the marketplace needs.

Bride and Groom

This series was photographed in New York City's Central Park during one of my summer workshops for photographers. The subject was suggested by my stock-photo agency. By focusing on this theme, I was able to show the class how to shoot commercial images for stock, as well as help my agency by producing saleable pictures.

The editors at The Image Bank decided that they needed more photographs of bride-and-groom situations. Their wedding files just weren't substantial enough. Particularly lacking were fully released photographs of very attractive brides and grooms that could be sold for commercial and advertising use. (There were plenty of pictures of real weddings in the files, but most of those were too posed for advertising sales.)

Setting up the workshop shoot with the agency's needs in mind, I hired six models (three couples) for the day. Renting a location van gave them a place to change clothes and provided the hair and makeup artist with a place to work. The van also held the wardrobe for a number of different situations.

We planned some of the shots, such as the ones of the couple in the gondola, a Venetian boat rented in the park, but basically we worked with ideas inspired by the light and the locations. Everything just happened naturally. I gave the models a few suggestions, shot a lot of film, and intentionally photographed as many variations as possible. It is crucial to frame subjects many ways—vertically, horizontally, up close, farther back, and so forth—in stock photography. This gives clients much more to choose from for their layouts, significantly increasing your sales potential.

Bride and Groom

Most of these pictures were taken with my 80-200mm zoom lens. The zoom feature was particularly handy for photographing the models in the gondola because when the gondola moved farther away, I could zoom in closer. I shot both Ektachrome 100 Plus film and Agfachrome 1000 RS film (for a grainy look), and I shot most situations both diffused and undiffused. It would have been great if I'd filmed the shoot in motion because The Image Bank is now selling film footage and the situation flowed so well. We had quite a crowd milling around as we took the pictures of Molly and Alan by the fountain (below). I think all the people thought they were watching a real bride and groom.

One last point: The bride's dress was purchased, not rented or borrowed, so we wouldn't have to worry about getting it wet or ruining it. The dress is now part of my prop collection. I'm sure I'll find a chance to use it again.

Children and Babies

Children are really fun to photograph for stock. As with adult models, I like to work with the same children repeatedly, making photographs around their personalities. Studio sessions with children are more controlled than working with them on location, but regardless, there are a lot of people involved: assistants, parents, my staff, and so forth. It can get hectic, but as with all of my stock shoots, I just go with the flow once the shooting starts. Believe me, that is the best approach with kids!

Child models are sometimes real professionals. I've photographed Nina often, and her aptitude for the job never ceases to amaze me. For the session with Nina sitting on the wicker chair (below), I set up various props, and she played with them. She enjoyed herself, and I just shot. She was on the set for over an hour and was more patient than some adults I've photographed. Of course, if she wanted a break or got tired she could have taken it, but she didn't—she was having fun.

Babies always top The Image Bank's request list, so my staff and I planned a day for a baby shoot. We organized it a week in advance to make sure that everything went smoothly. My assistant Laura called two agencies and explained that we needed babies of all nationalities for stock and that we

would pay each baby 150 dollars for two hours (plus the agency commission—model agencies add a 15 percent service charge on top of the fee for "handling" the booking and also take 20 percent from the model). At 9:30 A.M. on the day of the shoot, fifteen babies arrived at the studio. We picked five to photograph, one Korean, one Hispanic, one black, and two white. We started shooting at 10:00 A.M., as we already had a set lit and ready. We worked until noon, shooting from a list of poses, including a group picture (left), babies with props, and so forth, as well as whatever else happened.

If you can arrange it, try to cast and photograph babies on the same day in order to catch them in good spirits. Same-day casting and shooting also permits you to screen out babies with rashes, which come and go so quickly. The babies we used were really well behaved, especially Sasami, who is Korean. We had her come back to do a special picture (left) using only window light. She was such a pleasure to work with that I couldn't resist making this special set for her. The picture of Sasami alone won't sell as well as the others because it is highly stylized, not realistic. I made it more for myself and possibly for a card company, but to my surprise, The Image Bank put it in their catalog.

Children and Babies

The pictures of the children on the beach feature the youngsters whom my daughter Kendra babysits in Florida. They are a great bunch of kids and were game for an afternoon at the beach. We took the wardrobe, flags, buckets, and some snacks with us and had a good time. (The parents had all signed model releases for their children—I sent eight hundred dollars worth of prints to them.) It was a hazy day, which, with my soft filter, produced a misty effect in some of the pictures. The woman with the children is my younger

daughter, Jordana. Years ago, I had taken similar pictures of Jordana on a foggy beach. Those pictures have sold many times, and hopefully, some from this session will, too.

Kendra set up and assisted on the shoot. We photographed a lot of situations in a few hours and could have done more, but we ran out of light. I used one picture from this session on a promotional piece, and I'm going back to Florida soon to do another session with the kids. You are only as good as your subjects, so take advantage of the good ones!

Christmas in April

About nine months before Christmas, I received a request from my agency for new Christmas pictures. Advertising agencies generally start preparing their Christmas ads sometime in June or July, and my agency was preparing to have the right material on hand when the calls for Christmas pictures began arriving. Since I usually shoot my Christmas pictures at Christmastime, in April I'm ready for such requests from my agency.

For six or seven years I went every Christmas to my friends the Chitwoods' house in Connecticut to shoot Christmas pictures. Last year, however, I wasn't able to go, but my agency still expected me to deliver Christmas pictures. So, rather than lose sales related to promotion for the next Christmas, I decided to set up Christmas in April in my studio.

I built a little room set with a Christmas tree and hired some of my favorite models to create an "all-American" type of family. I felt that the scene needed something extra—more than just a mom, a dad, and kids—so I rented a cute, well-behaved dalmatian puppy for the day. He added a perfect touch to the scene (below).

After shooting the family in the Christmas set (top right), I photographed them against a gray seamless-paper backdrop (bottom right). I usually use a white backdrop, but this time I wanted a color with a little more "guts," and I was simply tired of white paper. Unlike the Christmas pictures, the picture made against the plain backdrop can sell year-round. Seamless backdrop pictures sell well because clients can easily insert type on the background or pull the people in the pictures off the background and put them anywhere in a layout.

Christmas in April

When you work with paid models, you should try to produce as many saleable pictures as possible. That is why I usually set up a backdrop, prelit and ready to go, right next to the set of the planned shoot. I move the models from set to backdrop for extra photographs, headshots, and so forth.

I covered, or photographed, the Christmas shoot in almost every possible way. I had the family dress in winter clothes, then in pajamas. I photographed the whole family, then just the kids, then the kids with

COURTESY HELLER & COHEN

the dog. I also photographed the parents alone in pajamas, with the dog and without the Christmas tree (bottom left). This picture later sold to Lipton Tea for use on a coupon published in Sunday newspapers (top left). I guess they liked that "American as apple pie" look.

In addition to working with the models as many ways as possible, I always try to use any sets I build more than once. It is crazy to go to all the cost and effort of building a set and then not take maximum advantage of it. You can't be in business as a stock photographer if you don't use everything at least twice, and maybe even more. So, rather than immediately tearing down the Christmas set, I hired a young African-American girl and boy to come in the next day, and I photographed them in the Christmas set (below). There is currently a definite lack of advertising-quality pictures of African Americans, which is sad but true. Knowing that, I try to fill the gap for advertisers who buy stock photography.

Christmas in April

A funny thing happened at the end of this shoot. When Matt, the male model for the "White Christmas" family, had finished for the day, his son, Jesse, came to meet him. I took one look at Jesse and said, "Matt, where have you been hiding this kid? He is great." So, I quickly dropped a gray mottled background in front of the seamless paper and photographed Matt with his son.

I also photographed Jesse alone, with the mottled backdrop, and in front of a large print of a girl I had hanging in the studio. Jesse was phenomenal. He fell right into the shoot and made the greatest expressions. I love Matt, and he is a great model—I use him all the time—but his son may be even better!

This all goes to show that you can't know in advance when a great opportunity for stock photography will present itself. But when the opportunity arises, you have to be ready—act fast and take advantage of it! By the way, I paid Jesse for the shoot and had him sign a model release.

Styling for Two Continents

My agency needed to fill a hole in a catalog they were putting together on the theme of "The Common Market." They wanted pictures of an upscale, affluent three-generation family who could be either European or American. Their exact instructions included the following condition: "no blonde mothers."

I called up casting agent Ester Johnston, and asked her to help set up a "family." She recommended two of my regular models from other shoots, J.D. and Gloria, to play the mother and father. I had already asked the Chitwoods to play the grandparents. Ester also found two "European-looking" children for the shoot. The kids she sent were perfect (only the little girl appears here). They were really brother and sister, they definitely look European, and their real mom was absolutely great.

When I contacted the models, I described the storyline: "An affluent family in a den or a library. Slightly formal, with dark colors." The children's mother brought along just the right clothes, as did J.D. and the Chitwoods. The red suit Gloria is wearing, however, came from my studio wardrobe. The gold buttons made it right for this situation.

I keep basic wardrobe items in the studio. When I see something that is classic and will be in style

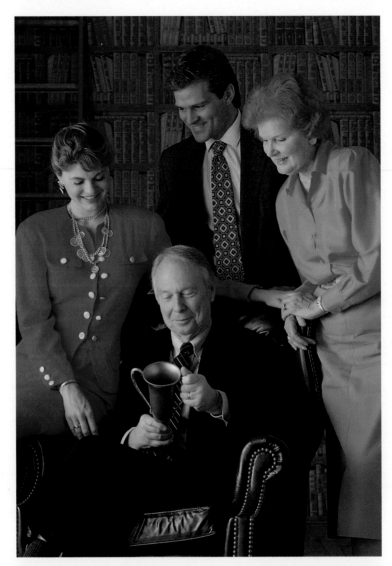

for a while, I buy it, whether or not I have a shoot in mind. I own many women's suits, men's ties and shirts, sweaters, and at least a hundred women's swimsuits in all colors. I also have lab coats, scarves, gloves, jewelry for headshots, and terrycloth robes for health-and-fitness pictures. I most often purchase women's clothes in size 8-10, large men's sweaters, and medium men's shirts. Occasionally, I buy something for a specific photograph and then return it.

To create a European-looking set, I covered some flats that I had in the studio with "faux bookshelf" wallpaper. It was perfect because I didn't want book titles that could be read—I just wanted the suggestion of bookshelves and deep, rich colors behind the subjects—and I found working with wallpaper a lot easier than building and stocking real shelves. To go with the library motif, I rented two chairs from a furniture store in my building: a maroon leather chair and a dark green leather chair, both classic styles. My agency also specifically asked me to include a trophy because they wanted to convey the idea that the father or the grandfather had won something. Out of millions of pictures in their files, they had none with someone holding a trophy. This may be hard to believe, but I swear it was true.

Styling for Two Continents

We spread the actual shooting over two days, which I often do in order to use different combinations of models and to keep everybody as fresh as possible. The first day I shot the three-generation family, with J.D. as the father and Mr. Chitwood as the grandfather (see page 116). The next day I had Mr. Chitwood come back and brought in another model, Matt, to play his son. They worked perfectly together, and Matt was ideal with the trophy. The pictures of them together are particularly good because they could be either "father and son" or "older and younger businessmen." Clients can use these pictures to convey either image.

In terms of lighting, these pictures aren't nearly as "open," or bright, as the Christmas shots. The lighting for the library scene is much more from the side, and the pictures look deeper and warmer, with much more shadow. They have a "richer" quality than the Christmas pictures, an atmosphere that fits the library situation and the idea of "old-money affluence." I'm very happy with the library shots. The light coming from the side and "falling off" quickly was very flattering to the models' faces, and the resulting skin tones are great.

As usual, I worked with the models on more than one set. Gloria, the "mom," has a great look. She can play anyone from nearly any part of the world, and, since I knew my agency's needs

by heart, I decided to photograph
her as a pregnant woman. I
quickly put up the French doors,
attached my "pregnant pillow"
to her waist, and shot several
rolls of film showing an American
or European pregnant mother.
One shot that worked well
included J.D. as the father and the
little girl recommended by Ester
as the daughter (below right). I
would never shoot this look for
myself, but I like the way the
pictures of her came out. They are
very good for what they are, and
I'm certain they will sell.

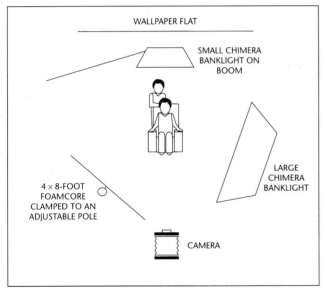

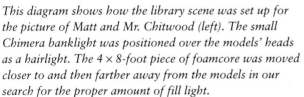

*This diagram shows how the library scene was set up for
the picture of Matt and Mr. Chitwood (left). The small
Chimera banklight was positioned over the models' heads
as a hairlight. The 4 × 8-foot piece of foamcore was moved
closer to and then farther away from the models in our
search for the proper amount of fill light.*

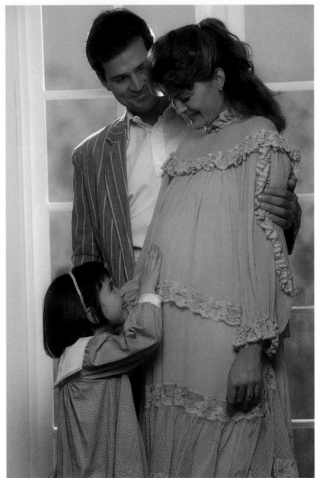

Everybody's Business

As mentioned earlier, good stock photographers carry their agency's request lists around in their subconscious minds and act on them when opportunities arise. That is what happened on this shoot. I'd done an assignment for which I'd built a den-like room in the studio. Creating the set was a lot of work for the single picture produced, and it would have been a shame to tear down the set right away. I decided to reprop it, install a different desk, and add a computer to use the set again for a day of stock photography.

Over the past few years, demand has increased for stock images of all nationalities, races, and ethnic groups. With that in mind, I opted to use the set as a backdrop for photographs of African-American and Asian models. I also wanted to work with one of my favorite models, Christine (see pages 44-47), who had called the week before saying that she needed pictures of herself in business environments. I asked her to come in, and I hired three other models, Conrad, Wanda, and Bing, through Ester Johnston. I also planned to use Valerie, my summer intern, in some shots. Valerie loved modeling, and she had a great smile. I did several shoots with her while she worked for me.

All the models wore their own clothes, except for Valerie, who wore a studio sweater. I photographed them in combinations of two, three, and four. I also did portraits

of Bing (top right), Christine (bottom right), Conrad (below), and the others. For each model, I changed the desk props a little. The set was lit with a large

banklight on one side, fill from the other side, and a hairlight above that I adjusted according to hair color. The desk light helped create a nice mood.

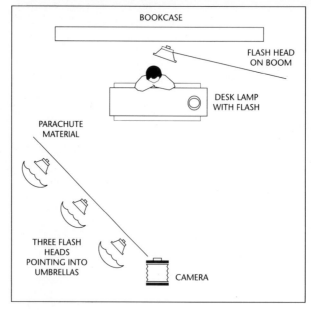

This diagram shows how we lit the picture of Conrad in the den scene. I used three flash heads reflecting into umbrellas lined up behind a parachute that provided diffusion. A flash head attached to a boom over Conrad's head was used as a hairlight. The lamp on the desk added fill light. No extra light was needed for the background.

BOOKCASE

FLASH HEAD ON BOOM

DESK LAMP WITH FLASH

PARACHUTE MATERIAL

THREE FLASH HEADS POINTING INTO UMBRELLAS

CAMERA

Everybody's Business

As soon as I finished with Christine and Bing, they left. Then I worked with Conrad, Wanda, and Valerie. I had them relate to each other like a family in their home (below). They changed clothes a couple of times. One of the pictures of Valerie (right) went into the next Image Bank catalog.

All the props in this series came from in my own studio prop area. I keep a number of vases, books, lamps, desk items, and a computer on hand. It saves time and money to have everyday props at your fingertips.

Wall Street Dynamos

This time, The Image Bank was looking for pictures of dynamic, active businessmen at work. I had a workshop coming up, so as usual I decided to kill two birds with one stone: fill the request and teach my class something about shooting for stock professionally. By now you can see that there is definitely a pattern in my thinking and the way I work, and it is about maximizing opportunity.

These pictures were all taken in a single day. I started out in the morning shooting in my studio. For models, I used several professionals who projected a great attitude, and John, who is a neighbor of mine. John is actually an actor, and he looks great in front of the camera. Sometimes he overacts, as in the shot with the telephone (bottom right), but I love working with him because he is willing to try anything at least once.

For the first set of studio shots, I used a mottled, gray-looking canvas background I've had for years. One of my favorite stylists painted it for me a long time ago, and I've since used it in many photographs. I also rented a huge chair from the furniture store downstairs, but it doesn't appear in any of these pictures.

The painted backdrop is actually very hard blue-gray and white. I wanted the photographs to have a much warmer, yellower, late-afternoon quality, so we used hot lights (tungsten spotlights) rather than flash to soften the appearance of both the backdrop and the models' faces. An advantage to working with painted backdrops is that you can change the way they look and their colors by using different types of lighting. You can

also move a backdrop closer or farther away from the models or use just a small section of it, which changes the backdrop's pattern. Most people won't notice that you reused a backdrop unless you tell them, and considering the money it costs to produce advertising-quality stock photographs, you should use the same backdrops over and over again.

The lighting setup for these studio shots is interesting. I put a slatted blind in front of the hot lights (which I love) to create shadow lines in imitation of light coming through a window. To copy this effect, hang a blind in front of lights and then move it closer and farther away until you form the shadows you want. I used a white 4 × 8-foot flat to provide some reflected fill light for the dark side of the models' faces. The lighting setup remained basically the same for all these shots; what changed were the combinations of models and props.

I used daylight film without any filtration with these hot lights, which is why the pictures have that warm, yellow-orange quality. If you are shooting with daylight film and don't want your pictures to look yellowish, put a blue gel in front of the hot lights. This will balance them for the film.

For the picture of the architect in his office (below), I simply turned a wall of my studio into the background. I also used hot lights here, but instead of projecting them through blinds, I put a loose window frame (without glass, left over from another shoot) in front of them. The set was really very simple—what makes the picture work is the warm lighting, and the model's talent.

Specialty Stock

Specialty-stock pictures fall outside the mainstream of stock photography. Unusual or unique images, they are likely to sell only to specialized markets. What you are paid for licensing the rights to these photographs should exceed standard stock-pricing guidelines that are based on how an image is used and an estimate of the number of people who see it. Specialty stock should sell for a slight premium. In most industries, a premium is placed on an authentically unique item. The same principle should apply in stock photography, and I believe that clients are gradually beginning to accept this idea.

An important category of specialty stock is what I call *slick stock*, which I usually do for my self-promotional pieces or my portfolio. I also publish such pictures in creative sourcebooks and direct-mail promotions. Slick-stock pieces are designed to catch the attention of art directors and show that you can handle a particularly difficult type of assignment. They may have complex lighting, very careful styling, or a technically unusual twist and are frequently big production shots, requiring a lot of planning and attention to detail. Slick-stock production is usually undertaken to create one specific picture rather than to cover a situation. The clothing, props, and camera angle are decided before the shoot.

Besides using slick-stock images for self-promotion, I almost always send them to The Image Bank. However, these pictures don't sell as well as those specifically designed for stock. Slick stock is good for a limited number of countries and industries, and only clients with specialized needs are likely to buy them.

Another important type of specialty image is *mood stock*. Mood photographs portray a particular emotion or atmosphere in a somewhat ephemeral or ambiguous manner. When I shoot mood stock, I don't show the models' faces—that would make the images too specific. You aren't likely to find these pictures on a real-estate brochure or a health-club flyer; instead, they sell as greeting cards or calendars.

Specialty Stock

Mood pictures often come out of shoots that I'd planned for something else. As such sessions progress, a mood develops, and I just work with the situation. Almost all the mood pictures in this chapter are the products of shoots begun for other purposes.

Specialty stock also includes a photographer's personal specialty.

Very tight beauty portraits (from, say, eyebrows to chin), either grainy or soft filtered, are my favorite specialty shots. I really enjoy photographing bits and pieces of faces if a model has excellent skin and features. Such pictures sell to cosmetic firms or pharmaceutical companies. Some photographers specialize in

shooting reenactments of scenes portrayed in old paintings. There are also photographers who specialize in shooting particular subjects, such as animals or trucks, and who have found a special niche in the stock business. The trick is to let clients who need a certain kind of stock photograph know that you have it.

Shooting for Self-Promotion

The slick-stock picture below is actually based on a similar self-promotional photograph I produced a number of years ago with a different couple in a black convertible (right). The earlier picture worked very well for me; it brought a good number of assignments and sold many times as stock.

When Dyna-Lite, an electronic-flash manufacturer, asked me to give a workshop at their factory in New Jersey, I decided to use the opportunity to redo the earlier car picture. I frequently reshoot pictures that have sold well but

NANCY BROWN
6 WEST 20 STREET
NYC 10011
(212) 924-9105
APA ASMP STOCK IMAGE BANK   SELECT STOCK IN STUDIO
REP IN CHICAGO DOUG BROOKS (312) 642 3280

become dated in terms of clothing and fashion, or that have been oversold. Reshooting subjects helps guarantee that my pictures will continue to sell. Also, this practice is more ethical than what some stock photographers do, which is to produce replicas of bestselling photographs taken by other photographers.

For this shot I hired a male model friend, Fred, who had the right looks and owned a cute red convertible and an elegant tuxedo. As I've said many times in this book, you have to be quite ingenious to keep costs down when you produce stock photography. It is never guaranteed that a picture will sell, and any income you make will be months in the future (at least). So taking advantage of such opportunities as Fred and his great car makes sense. Cutting costs also makes the whole process more challenging and personally satisfying.

The diagram shows how the car picture was set up and lit. However, it doesn't explain how long my workshop students worked at getting the lighting just right or how uncomfortable and cramped the shooting platform was. A clean car is highly reflective, and to photograph one well, you have to use a very large and even light source. The Dyna-Lite factory had high, dark ceilings, so we suspended white seamless paper over the car to bounce the flash onto the scene, rather than using a bunch of individual umbrellas or flash heads.

My students went crazy trying to get the reflections in the car to match perfectly on both sides. Finally, I told them to stop; they were close enough. If the reflections had been too perfect, the picture would have appeared plastic and contrived. Another problem involved keeping the windshield clear of any reflections in order to show the legs of the models through it. This was solved after much trial and error. We moved a large black card back and forth until the black card was reflected in the windshield. This made the windshield appear clear.

In the end Dyna-Lite used this photo for an advertisement (left), and I came away from the workshop with some great stock photos, which made recreating the car picture more than worth the effort.

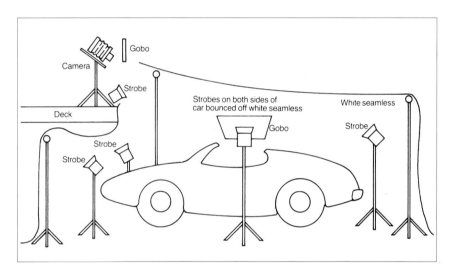

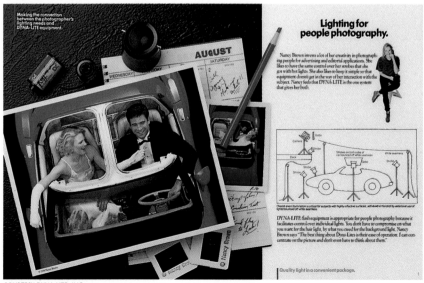

COURTESY DYNA-LITE, INC.

Color Plus Shape Equals Mood

The picture of the figure dressed in red was taken at the Knoll Estate on Long Island, New York. We traveled there during a workshop so my class could experience a shoot on location and see how I work away from the studio. On the estate grounds, fantastic old gardens were filled with interesting little areas, secluded corners, and stately, manicured walkways and paths.

I had bought the red cape a few months earlier, knowing it would be an ideal prop, but I hadn't yet found the perfect use for it. As the class and I were walking through the gardens looking for locations to shoot, we came across huge, carefully trimmed, round bushes. Their shape vaguely reminded me of something, but it took a while for me to decide exactly what. Suddenly I realized that they looked like a figure in a cape wearing a hood. It had rained recently, and the gardens were very green. In my mind, the image came into focus—the vivid green color would contrast perfectly with my red cape! I ran back to the van (which was stuffed with clothing and props), rummaged around, pulled out the cape, ran back to the scene, and started taking pictures.

I like this photograph a lot, and as a matter of fact, I have a large print of it hanging in my studio. People who visit me often make comments about it. Despite the fact that the colors and shapes are great, and the scene has an evocative quality, I'm not certain it will sell well as stock. If it ever does sell, it will probably be for reproduction on a specialty item, such as a poster or calendar. It is the rare client, however, who buys the rights to a stock picture simply because it is a good picture. The picture might also sell as a book cover, perhaps to a murder mystery or a horror story (I hope not!).

The picture of the figure in a hooded white cape (right) is also ambiguous. This picture was shot

in the studio against a painted backdrop. The "snow" on the floor is actually crumpled white cloth. If you look closely at the picture, you can tell that the snow is fake; however, that doesn't bother me. One of the reasons for this photograph is that it is fabricated. It is a representation of a fantasy.

Beginning photographers frequently make two mistakes when using painted scenic backdrops. The first mistake is trying to make them look real. Painted backdrops aren't meant to look real. They are meant to look like paintings, to be artistic representations, stylized interpretations of scenes. If you understand that and use this type of backdrop to add flavor, feeling, and mood, your pictures will be much better than if you try using them to produce a picture that looks real.

The second mistake is attempting to light scenic backdrops as if they could be illuminated with light of the photographer's choosing. The vast majority of painted backdrops are painted already lit—that is, a direction and type of light already exists in the painting. The correct approach is to illuminate the backdrop evenly, and then match the light striking the subjects with the direction of the light in the painting. You can, however, change the colors or tones of painted backdrops by putting gels on your lights or by the type of lighting you choose. Many photographers modify the effect of backdrops this way. You can use tungsten lights to warm the colors and make the backdrop appear to be a late afternoon or evening scene, or you can put slightly blue gels in front of electronic flashes to make the backdrop's colors colder and harder. I frequently play with the colors of rented backdrops in this fashion, especially when I rent them more than once or use them for more than one photograph.

Uncommon Beauty: Identical Twins

These pictures are specialty stock not because they involved elaborate production or are unusual in terms of approach and feeling, but because they have a very uncommon subject. How often do you see identical twins, much less beautiful identical female twins at just the right age for modeling, and with magnificent red hair?

I met Tammy and Tanya in Canada, and invited them to come to New York City for some photography sessions. I flew them down a few months later, and they stayed in my apartment. We worked for a week straight, and I photographed them in an incredible variety of situations. I only have room to show a few of the results here, but I must say that they approached everything as real professionals, as well as real sports.

The photograph of Tammy and Tanya sitting in the sunlight (top right) was set up near my studio's back windows when the sun was shining. It was the first shot I did the week they were in New York. They were wearing very little makeup and looked quite natural—it was a good way to begin. As the week went by, I covered many situations and loved shooting them all. I hardly gave any directions to the twins because they seemed to be in their own world and were in such harmony that it was like shooting one person.

The tight headshot (bottom right) was designed with a mauve color scheme to blend with the models' coloring. It was a great color for the twins. I took this shot in both grainy and nongrainy versions. With their skin, the nongrainy approach worked best.

The birthday party shot (below) is a good example of how I strategize when shooting for stock. When you think of twins, what is the first thing that comes to mind? Probably the fact that they were born on the same day. That is a perfect stock-photography concept. Birthday parties are easily pictured, yet they have numerous connotations (this picture would be perfect for a client celebrating the second anniversary of a product). In stock photography, the simplest ideas are often the best.

At the end of the week, I realized that I had photographed Tammy and Tanya separately only once. I had made enough pictures of them to fill a book, and I could have shot more. They were a pleasure to work with, and I missed them when they went back to Canada.

Experimenting with Computers

The stock-photography industry is evolving as a result of computer technology. Today, it is possible, and increasingly practical, to combine and alter photographs though the use of a computer. With the touch of a few buttons, you can change backgrounds, remove and retouch imperfections or unwanted items, and create entirely new images that appear to be ordinary photographs taken in camera. Every day, more users of stock photographs are manipulating images this way.

The subject of computer technology and photography is interesting and complex enough for a book of its own. However, my point here is that computer technology is rapidly and radically affecting stock photography and the types of photographs produced for stock. How this technology will be used, and what its ultimate effect on the industry will be, is uncertain. Experts in stock photography (and in many allied industries, such as publishing, printing, and advertising) have closely monitored the development of computer technology for years now, and I'm not sure that any of them have a definite answer.

What you see on these pages is a little experiment with computer imaging that I did for myself. I wanted to see if what I had been reading and hearing about

combining images was true—it was. The final picture (below) is a relatively simple combination of two photographs, and it is probably a more saleable image than the originals. The first picture, a nude of Kim (top left), was taken in my studio. The other picture, fountains in Central Park (bottom left), had been in my files for years. Using a computer, I decided to put the fountains in the background behind the nude of Kim.

Combining the images didn't turn out to be easy or cheap. I had to have one company convert my original photographs into computer information, and then at another, I worked closely with someone who knew how to combine the images in a way that looked real to me. Then, I had to go to yet another company to have the computer file output at a quality level that I considered similar to an original photograph. Still, this was a fascinating experiment and experience. I love learning about new things. And to me, these pictures show that the future possibilities for the creation of stock photographs are mind-boggling. What do you think?

Final Notes

My Photography Equipment

I'm a sincere believer in using and carrying the smallest amount of photography equipment necessary to perform a job properly. Keeping your equipment as basic and simple as possible allows you to concentrate on what really matters—your photographs. The last thing any professional photographer needs is more gadgets to break, extra buttons and knobs to learn, or more cases and bags filled with valuables that might stray.

My standard camera is a Nikon F4, equipped with a motor drive, which I use probably 90 percent of the time. My favorite lens is a Nikkor 80–200mm zoom that I find ideal both in the studio and on location. In the past, I used a whole battery of fixed-focus lenses, but when I found the Nikkor 80–200mm zoom to be as sharp as fixed-focus lenses, it became my real workhorse. It is much simpler and more practical to work with one lens than to switch lenses with every change of position or frame. The zoom is a heavy lens, but the weight of that big lens helps you to hold the camera steady.

I prefer to take exposure readings with a handheld meter rather than use the exposure meter built into my camera. I trust the handheld readings more—although photographer friends tell me that I'm being old-fashioned, and every time I've used the camera's meter the results have been just fine. The handheld meter I use today is a Minolta IV. I use it to measure the light falling on a scene rather than the light reflecting off the models. My assistant also carries a meter, and while shooting, we constantly compare readings. We shout the readings off as the light's or model's position changes.

When I go on location shoots, I always bring along at least one additional F4 and two 80–200mm zoom lenses as backups. The last thing I need is to bring some great models to a great location and find out that a piece of my equipment isn't working. For the same reason, I always pack a second exposure meter and plenty of spare batteries for both the cameras and meters.

I usually bring along a 35–105mm zoom lens when I go on location—just in case I have to work in close quarters—and a 24mm lens for wide-angle shots. And, of course, I pack my favorite filters (most notably a #1 diffusion filter and a polarizer). All of this fits very neatly in one medium-sized Haliburton case that is easy to carry and locate in a crowd.

I rarely switch back and forth between camera bodies, handing one off to an assistant to reload, as some photographers do. I've always preferred to load my own film. That way I am certain it is loaded properly. If it isn't, there is no one else to blame but myself. I also hardly ever set my motor drives in the continuous-firing mode. I shoot a lot of film, but I like to control when the shutter fires.

I make up for the sensible amount of photography equipment I carry by lugging around masses of film, clothing, and props. I always bring much more film than I think I'll need when I go on location, and I usually use more than I expected. It makes no sense to run out of film when things are going well; although the cost of film and processing does add up, it is an expense I never skimp on. When it comes to stock photography, I believe that it is nearly impossible to shoot too much film.

I always bring a huge wardrobe and many props to a location shoot. I plan a number of outfits to cover the situations I expect to shoot, but I also want to be able to take advantage of unexpected opportunities, locations, and ideas that may crop up. Sometimes I have so many outfits and props with me that you'd imagine I was opening a second-hand store. My van gets so packed that there is almost no room for the models and crew.

Getting Model Releases Signed

The question I'm asked most often during my workshops and seminars is: "How do I get people to sign a release for stock?" The answer is quite simple. I pay my models—or, in a few cases, I trade photographs—for a signed model release.

When I began shooting for stock fifteen years ago, it was a much smaller, more intimate industry. Many photographers—myself included—often worked on a verbal basis with models. The agreement for a stock shoot was that when and if the pictures sold, the models would be paid either a fee or a percentage of the sale. Photographers often didn't pay anything at the time of a shoot. Stock shoots were seen as entirely speculative on the part of both the photographers and the modeling talent. As a result, photographers frequently didn't ask the models to sign any paperwork regarding rights to the images.

In the early days, The Image Bank used three types of release stamps on their slides. An "R" stood for a signed release, "PR" stood for a signed and paid release, and "PRA" stood for "paid release available," meaning than when a sale was made, the talent would be contacted, paid, and then sign a release for that particular sale. Now only "R" photos are accepted.

Today, with photographs selling all over the world, such a loose system no longer makes logistical sense. There usually isn't enough time or any easy way to go back to the model. As a result, the only kind of photographs that are really practical for stock agencies to market are completely released pictures. For years, I've given my agency only what I refer to as "clean and clear" photographs. All my stock photos are completely released, and the models have been paid for the time and work they put into the shoot.

Paying someone when they sign a release and having some sort of financial transaction is extremely important from a legal point of view. It is the exchange of money that really seals and solidifies a model or property release, even if it is only the payment of a token sum. The exchange of money means that the model has a much less valid claim for further payment. Paying your models makes producing stock much more costly, but you must spend money to produce top-quality and bestselling stock images.

Another common arrangement, especially between beginning photographers and models, is to agree to a trade. The photographer exchanges photography services for a signed release from the models. The photographer is allowed to market the pictures as stock, and the models receive top-quality photographs taken by a professional for their portfolios. I do this occasionally, and I've found that it often works out quite well for both parties.

Two words of caution about trades, however. First, be certain your models understand that signing a release for stock means that the pictures may be published almost anywhere and that you don't really have any control over their use. Some models may justifiably have a problem with this. While it is extremely unlikely that there will ever be any problem, a model must understand exactly what it means to sign a release.

Second, don't promise to give models photographs from the shoot and then turn around and say that there are some they cannot have. I always allow my models to chose any photograph they wish, even ones that I consider the very best. If they choose images I consider to be "seconds," I frequently give them the original slides. If they choose what I consider to be the very best shots, I pay for the cost of making duplicates so both the models and I have copies.

When one of my stock photographs sells for an especially high price or large usage, I frequently contact the models in that picture and pay them a small bonus—even though legally I don't have to do this. I feel that is only fair, and it also makes good business sense. You need great models to take great stock photographs, and happy models are the best models. I'm in business for the long term, and I want all the models I work with on stock shoots to be more than glad to work with me again—especially when the pictures of those particular models sell well.

Professional Photographers' Organizations

If you are truly serious about professional photography, I strongly suggest that you join either the ASMP or APA, two major professional photographers' organizations. You'll learn a lot during the meetings, seminars, and lectures these associations hold, and they provide the invaluable opportunity to meet and talk with other professional photographers. They are the best way I know of keeping your finger on the pulse of local business, learning industry trends, and picking up useful tips.

I've been involved with both ASMP and APA for many years and have served on the board of directors of both organizations. Doing so has taken a lot of time and plain hard work, but it has helped my career and, more important, given me a feeling of having returned something to the industry that has been so good to me. Helping other professional photographers—including those I've never met—has made being involved a real pleasure.

ASMP

The ASMP (The American Society of Media Photographers) has over 5,400 professional photographers as members and active chapters in virtually every major city and region of the United States. The organization was established in 1944, and its purpose is "to promote high professional and artistic standards and to further the professional interests of its membership by disseminating information on a range of subjects and concerns."

The ASMP is open to virtually all types of professional photographers, but there are various categories of membership, and you do have to be sponsored by present members to join. For more information, contact the chapter nearest you or the ASMP's national headquarters in New York City. The address and telephone number are:

ASMP
419 Park Avenue South
New York, NY 10016
Tel: (212) 889–9144

APA

The APA (Advertising Photographers of America) is a newer, smaller organization than the ASMP. It is designed to address the needs and concerns of photographers specializing in advertising work. At present, there are only chapters in major metropolitan areas, but a number of photographers based in other parts of the country are members of those chapters. The best way to find out more about APA and learn how to contact the chapter nearest you is to call or write the association in New York. The address and phone number are:

APA
27 West 20th Street
New York, NY 10011
Tel: (212) 807–0399

Books

My focus in this book has been on photographing people for stock—understanding the types of photographs that sell best, setting up production shoots, working with models, and taking saleable photographs. While I've touched on many other aspects of earning an income as a stock photographer, it hasn't been the purpose of this book to discuss every aspect of stock photography in detail.

There is much about the business aspects of stock photography that you have to know in order to be truly successful—information and techniques related to marketing, promotion, legal issues, taxes, pricing, distribution, and so forth. If you are serious about making money and developing a long-term career as a stock photographer, I recommend that you read the following; they are some of the best books about the business aspects of professional and stock photography available.

ASMP Stock Photography Handbook, 2d ed.
This book is as close to the stock-photographer's bible as you can get. It discusses the legal and business issues in depth, offers suggestions for pricing and

resolving disagreements, provides circulation figures for many major magazines, covers crucial copyright questions, contains many useful forms, and much more. It is a very valuable reference book at an extremely moderate price. If you can't find it on sale in your local camera store, lab, art-supply store, or bookstore, you can order it directly from the ASMP.

ASMP Copyright Guide for Photographers
A "white paper" rather than a book, this brochure is the best concise guide to what every professional photographer needs to know about copyright. It includes information on copyright basics, registration, proper notice, work for hire, fair use, and much more. It is available from the ASMP.

Business and Legal Forms for Photographers, by Tad Crawford
Besides including sample contracts and forms to meet almost every situation a photographer could run across, the book has useful information on contracts, negotiating, and how to locate good attorneys and resource groups. The book is available from Amphoto. To order it, call (908) 363-5679.

Negotiating Stock Photo Prices, by Jim Pickerell
This is very useful guide to exactly what the title says. The book covers a comprehensive list of uses for photographs, and it has a great discussion of the many variables

that need to be considered and agreed on for a successful transaction to take place between client and photographer. It is available directly from the author. Write him a letter to receive a current order form: Jim Pickerell, 110 Frederick Avenue, Suite A, Rockville, MD 20850.

Selling Stock Photography: How to Market Your Photographs for Maximum Profit, by Lou Jacobs, Jr. This concise guide provides business know-how in the fastest growing area of commercial photography, with advice on shooting for stock, editing pictures, marketing, negotiating agreements, and choosing a stock agency. The book is published by Amphoto. To order it, call (908) 363-5679.

Shooting for Stock, by George Schaub
This book features up-to-date analysis on how to create, organize, and market photographs. It also includes step-by-step information on tools and techniques, along with profiles of successful stock photographers, lists of agencies, marketing sources, business techniques, and organizations. The book is published by Amphoto. To order it, call (908) 363-5679.

Stock Photo Forms, by Michel Heron
This book contains seventeen useful forms ready to be photocopied or taken to a printer, plus a list of resources, such as books and

organizations. The book is slim but worth the very low price. The book is available from Amphoto. To order it, call (908) 363-5679.

Finding a Stock-Photography Agency to Represent You

Some stock-photography agencies are constantly on the lookout for new photography talent, while others practically refuse to talk to, much less see, photographers whom they don't know.

Agencies have different policies about what they want to see from new photographers and how they chose who they wish to represent. Today, almost all good agencies are extremely selective in whom they decide to represent. Virtually every stock agency requires that a photographer sign an exclusive contract.

Before you call a stock agency and try to make an appointment to show your work, you should do a little research. Find out everything you can about that particular agency. Ask your photographer and art-director friends if they know anything about the agency. Call the agency's main number and ask if they have any printed material about the agency that they could send to you. Even drive or walk by their offices so that you have some idea what size they are and what type of

Final Notes

neighborhood they picked. That can tell you a lot.

Doing your "homework" will impress the person who finally sees you. It can also help you to avoid wasting an agency's (and your own) time. It would be futile, for example, to show lifestyle photographs to someone at an agency that specializes in architectural photography.

A stock agency wants photographers who will really produce. They want someone who will give them lots of good images frequently. Every photographer an agency has takes work, requires staff time, fills filing space, and is an administrative and accounting expense. Simple business sense says that these costs are best expended on photographers who make the agency good money. And, from a more emotional point of view, agencies generally want their photographers to speak well of the agency. Low-selling photographers are less likely to be happy photographers, even if lower sales are their own fault.

The last thing a stock agency wants is a roster of stock photographers who only take pictures when they are on vacation and submit small batches of new material only once or twice a year when the feel like it. Agencies, and photographers as well, just don't make money that way.

To illustrate my point, here is a direct quote from the latest of many letters, bulletins, and publications my stock-photo agency sends me every month: "DO THE RIGHT THING! Expedite editing, expedite your images. DO NOT send submissions that contain old and outdated imagery, resubmitted images that have not been separated and noted as such, or submissions that have not been tightly pre-edited (by louping each image and removing any images that are out of focus, damaged, or otherwise technically deficient)."

The tone of that paragraph is very serious. But you have to be serious in business today, and you have to be tough when you receive tens (if not hundreds) of thousands of new photographs a month. What my agency is saying is that they want their photographers to act like professionals and business people who see stock photography as their main business, not as an afterthought.

I provide my agency with between a thousand and fifteen hundred new slides a month, every month. Organizing my work is not as exciting as shooting, but I consider editing, labeling, packaging, and sending in my slides to be part of my job. It certainly has everything to do with how much income I receive from my stock photography. If my pictures don't make it into the marketplace, they cannot sell, so I make sure I submit new slides every month. Some months I may have to be hard at work editing a group of slides while my friends go out, but personally I think the many benefits stock photography provides me make this small final effort worthwhile.

Some of the largest and most reputable stock agencies in the United States are members of PACA (the Picture Agency Council of America), a trade association. All the members of PACA are independent (and in come cases fiercely competitive) companies. These agencies vary widely in size, the types of markets they serve, and the types of work and photographers they represent. Some have material from hundreds (if not thousands) of photographers, and some represent less than half a dozen photographers. In addition, a few of these agencies handle only historical material or provide marketing services for specific publishing companies. Remember, it is best to do a little research on agencies before approaching them.

A number of these agencies have offices or representatives in more than one American city. A list of addresses for each agency's U.S. headquarters can be obtained by writing to:

PACA
c/o Michael Jungert
The Image Bank/Chicago
510 N. Dearborn Street
Chicago, IL 60610

Index

Index